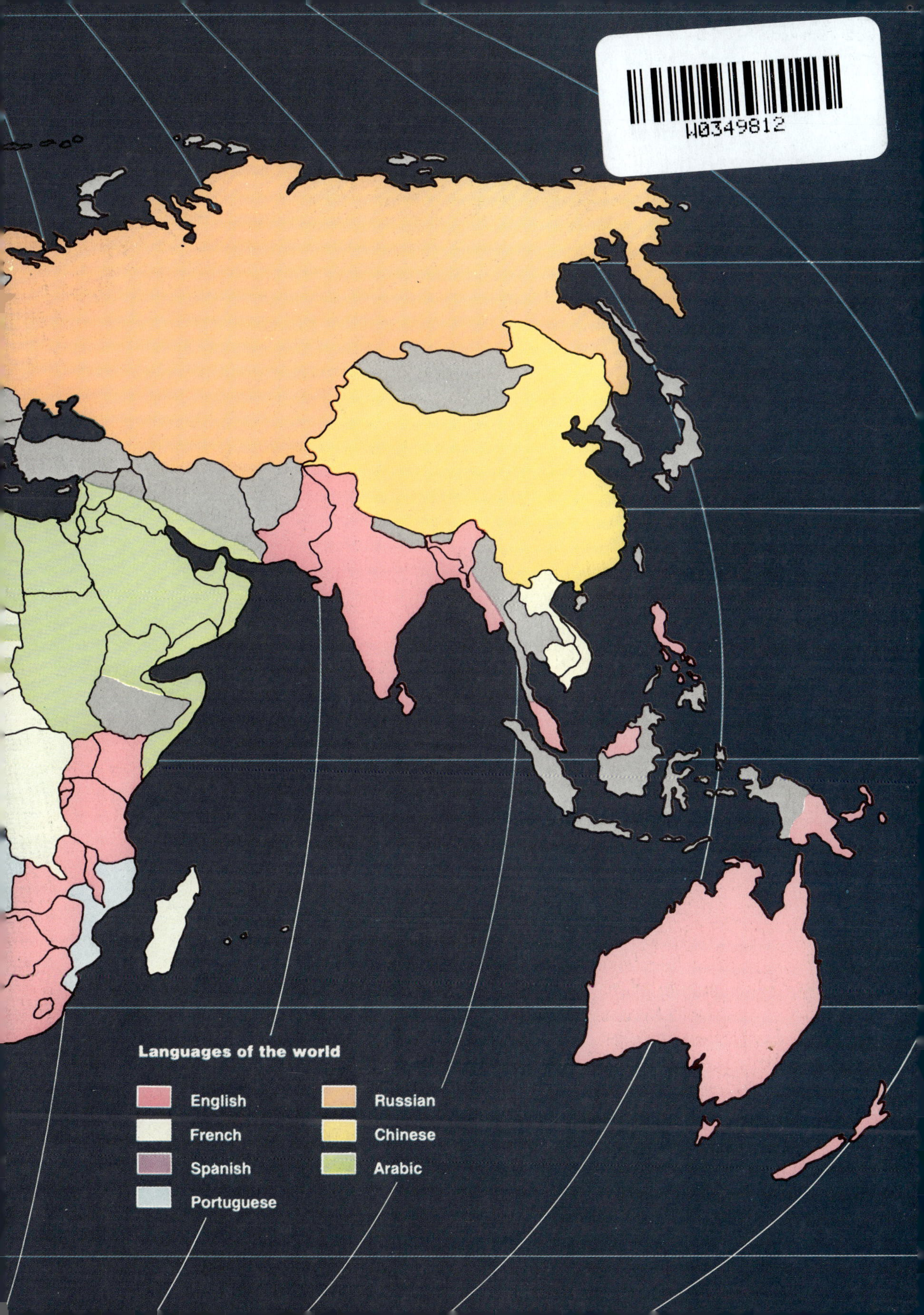
Languages of the world
English
French
Spanish
Portuguese
Russian
Chinese
Arabic

CONTACTS

Englischlehrwerk für die Klassen 5–10

Herausgegeben von

Hans-Eberhard Piepho
und Lothar Bredella

unter Mitarbeit von

Margie Berns
Vera Breuer
Werner Genzlinger
Lore Gerster
Louanna Heuhsen
Rainer Iwen
Delia Krause
Jutta Krüger
Dieter Mulch
Colin Oakley
Harald Ponader
Heike Rautenhaus
Franz Wenisch

CONTACTS 9

Projects I Basic Course

9. Schuljahr

für Hauptschulen
und Gesamtschulen

bearbeitet von

Hans-Eberhard Piepho
Margie Berns
Werner Genzlinger
Louanna Heuhsen
Franz Wenisch

VERLAG FERDINAND KAMP BOCHUM

Umschlaggestaltung: Paul Wohlrab

Illustrationen: Paul Wohlrab
Hartwig Bertram

Zu diesem Schülerbuch sind ein Lehrerkommentar, ein Arbeitsheft, Tonbandkassetten und Folien erschienen.

ISBN: 3—592—**36900**—8

Genehmigt für den Gebrauch in Schulen:

Hamburg Lernbuchliste
Hessen IV B 6 — 074/221
Niedersachsen 2063 — 82 — 221 — 3224/3
Nordrhein-Westfalen IA 5.82—11 Nr. 1.858/81
Rheinland-Pfalz 944 B Tgb. Nr. 679/82

Herstellung: Verlag Ferdinand Kamp GmbH & Co, KG Bochum

2 3 4 5 6 / 87 86 85 84 83
Die erste Zahl nennt die derzeitige Auflage und die letzte Zahl das Erscheinungsjahr.

Experiments

Your choice

Project 1

Starters

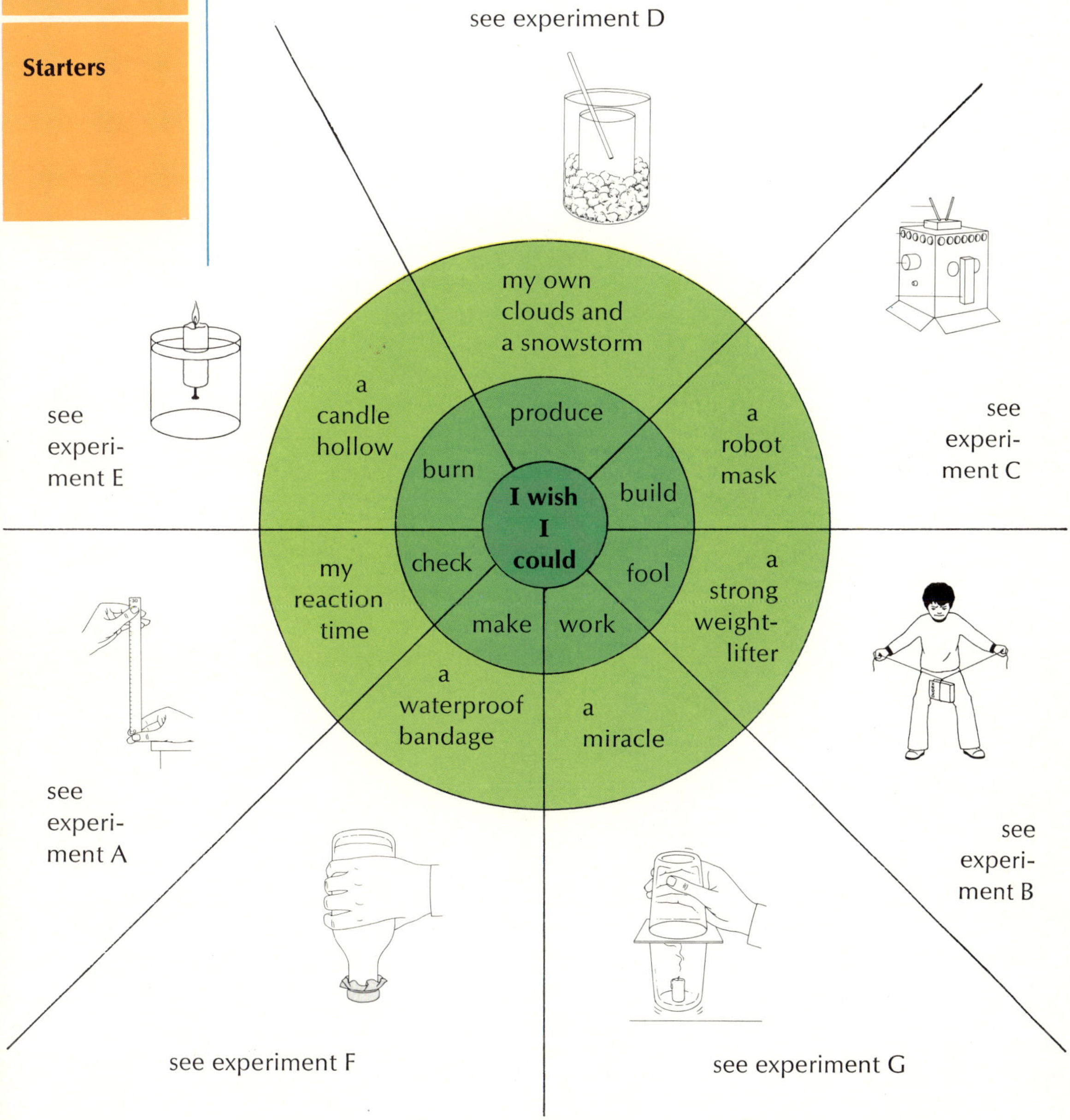

Look at the experiment instructions.
Try and tell your friends about them.

Before you start: Things to make things

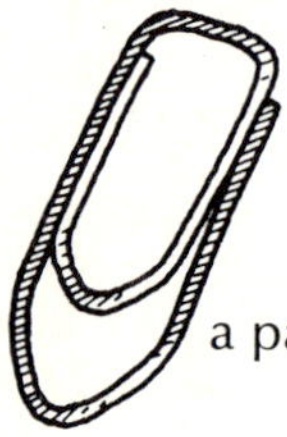
a paper clip
10 = 1 point

nails

25 = 1 point

a needle

1 = 4 points

a spool of thread

= 15 points

a pair of scissors
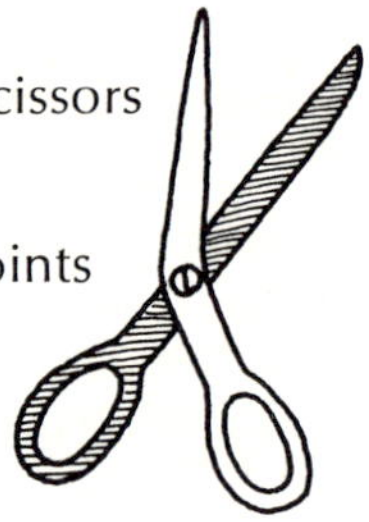
1 = 20 points

a screwdriver

1 = 10 points

cardboard + paper etc.
5 = 1 point

boards
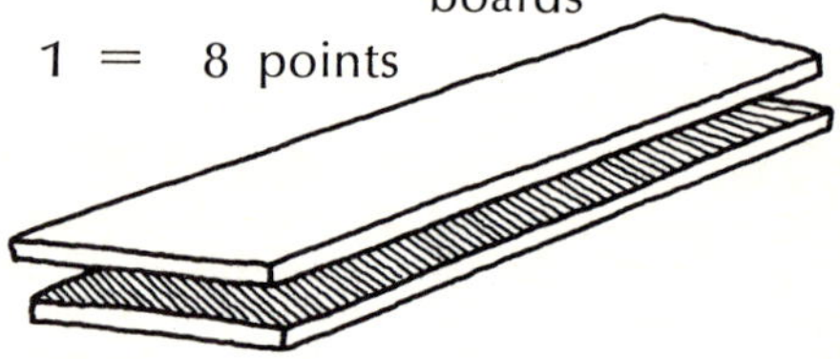
1 = 8 points

pins
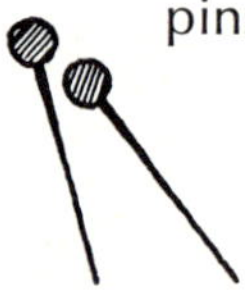
35 = 1 point

scotch tape

1 spool = 40 points

drawing pins

40 = 2 points

some rubber bands

25 = 1 point

a letter punch
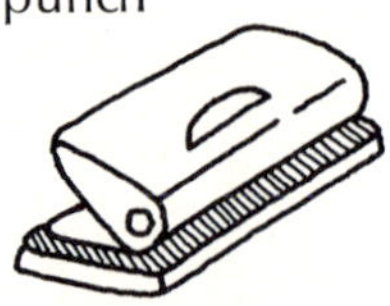
1 = 15 points

some glue

1 = 15 points

a pen knife
1 = 20 points
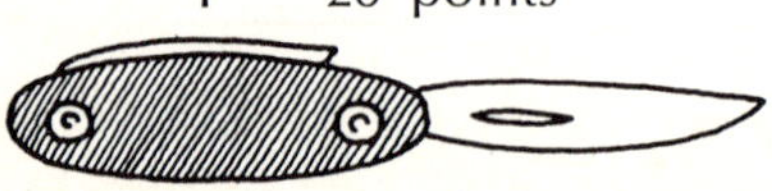

A group contest

Form 3 or 4 groups of about 7 members.

The task: Who can build the most fantastic dream castle in 25 minutes?

What you need: – A central depot with the objects above.

What you do:
- Discuss what you need and what you can afford (Each group has 80 points).
- Send two members to the depot with a list of things.
- Start building.
- Return tools and surplus materials.

Your teacher and two tellers are the jury.

The jury has a hundred points to give.

Example:

Castle 1	Castle 2	Castle 3	Castle 4
50 points	20 points	15 points	15 points

= First prize Castle 1.

Extra points: The group may tell a story about the castle in English. The jury can give another 100 points for the stories.

Example:

	Group 1	Group 2	Group 3	Group 4
castle	50 points	20 points	15 points	15 points
story:	5 points	20 points	50 points	25 points
	55	40	65	40

Winner: Group 3

some string

5 m = 12 points

the flat pliers

1 = 20 points

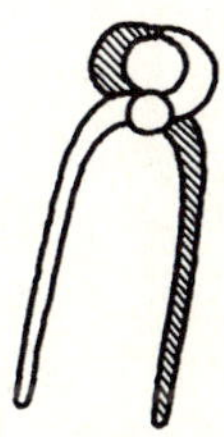

paper fastener

40 = 2 points

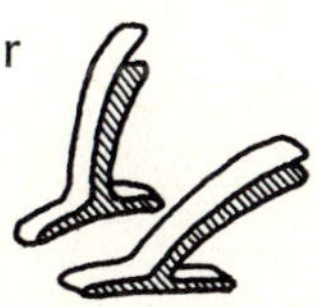

the pincers

1 = 20 points

You have chosen one of the following experiments.

Join the other classmates who have chosen the same experiment. Study the instructions.

Can your experiment be done in the classroom?

Or should you better try it at home?

Project 1

Experiments

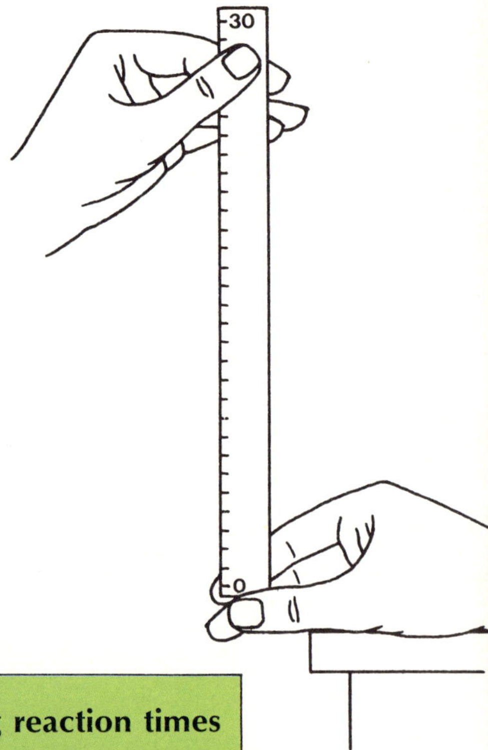

1

Experiment A: Testing reaction times

How fast are your reactions?
Here is a simple test to measure the time of your reaction.

First find a friend to test you.
Put your arm on a table with your hand over the edge.

Your friend holds a ruler at the upper end. You have your thumb and forefinger at the zero mark – but you do not touch the ruler.

Your friend suddenly lets go. You close your hand to catch it as quickly as you can.

The mark on the ruler where your thumb and finger have caught the ruler shows your reaction time.

Let all your English group members do the reaction test.

. . .'s rating   is/was . . .

Number of centimetres the ruler falls	Reaction time in hundredths of a second	Rating
2 4	7 9	Excellent
6 8 10	11 13 14	Very good
12 14 16 18	16 17 18 19	Good
20 22 24	20 21 22	Fair
26 28 30	23 24 25	Poor

Put it in writing

Write a short report.

What happened?

good sentence starters	**sub-ject**	**verbs** (past tense, of course)	**the objects etc.**
At the beginning First After that Now Then Next Afterwards Later Finally In the end	I he she we they nobody	looked for put held had didn't let go closed caught (didn't catch) had a reaction time of	. . . .

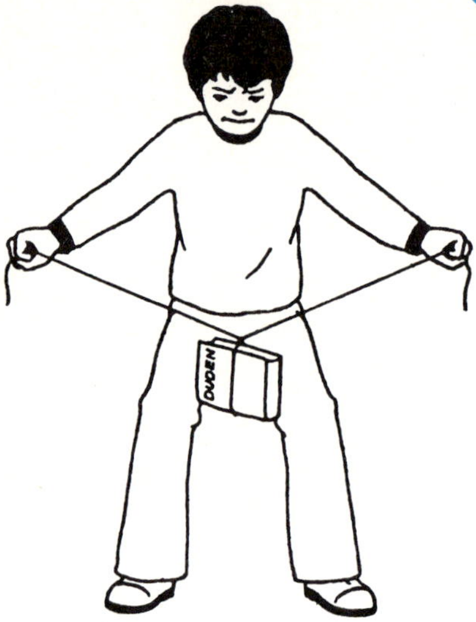

2

Experiment B:
How to fool a strong weight-lifter

Of course, you have big girls and boys with strong muscles in your group.

Test your muscles.
First you get a thick book –
perhaps a big dictionary or an atlas.

Tie round it a piece of strong string about 1.50 metres long.

Now hold one end
of the string in each hand and pull as hard as you can. Try to make the two halves of the string a horizontal line. Can anyone get the line straight?
If so, write us his or her name and the weight of the books in grammes.

Put it in writing

Write a report by using the list below.

good sentence starters	**sub-ject**	**verbs** (past tense, of course)	**the objects etc.**
At the beginning First After that Now Then Next Afterwards Later Finally In the end	he she I they we	fetched tied held pulled tried made (couldn't make)	a thick book . . .

Now write short instructions for your friend to try the experiment on other people.

good sentence starters	**subject**	**verbs**	**objects**
At the beginning First Then	you	fetch tie hold pull try	. . . .

3

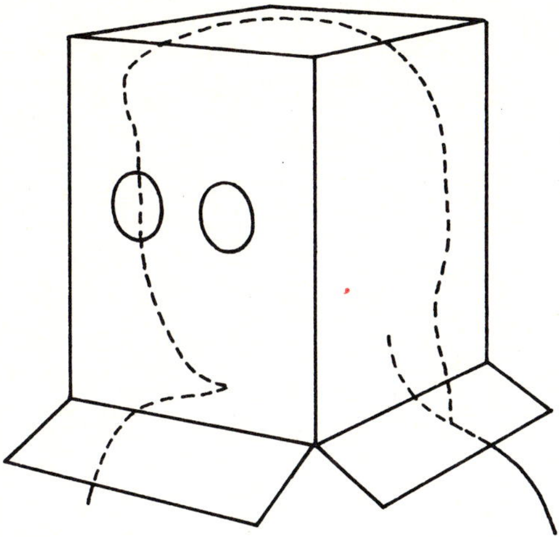

Experiment C: Making a robot mask

You need: a large cardboard box to fit on your head,
drinking straws,
bottle tops,
toilet roll tubes,
a toothpaste carton,
a tea packet,
a pencil or a felt pen,
strong glue,
paint,
a pair of scissors.

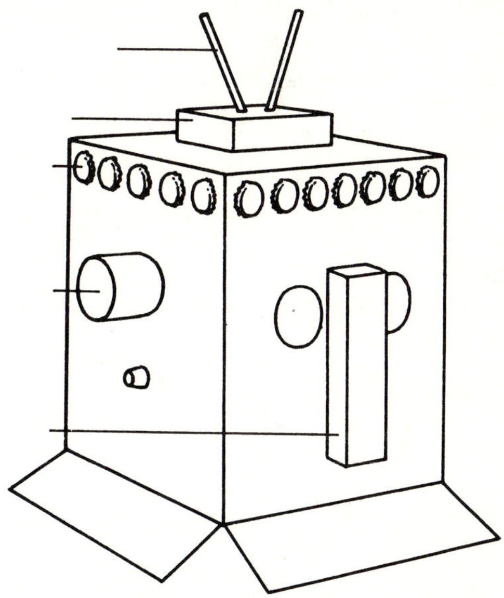

Talk about your experiments

. . . finished it more . . .
. . . did it less . . .

. . . told his story . . .
. . . talked about his experiment . . .

. . .	finished	his . . .	as quickly as . . .	
	made	her . . .	not as	nicely as . . .
	built			well as . . .
				carefully as . . .

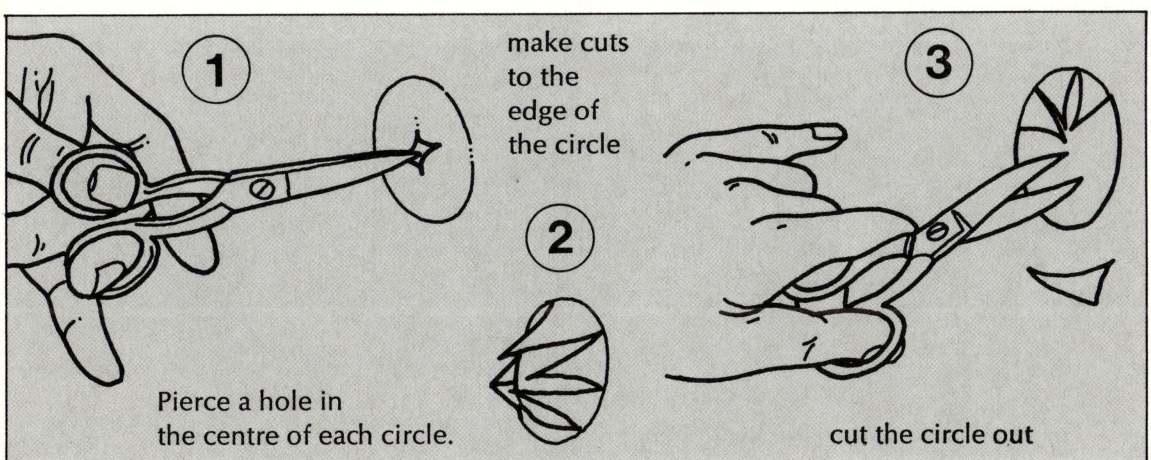

Task **Here are some sentences.**

Can you put them in the right order to make a good instruction text?

Use strong glue to add the nose, the ears and the antenna box.

Put it over your head with the flaps down on your shoulders.

A very clever idea: put a small cassette recorder in the antenna box to play space music.

Write: "Made in . . ." or "Made by . . ." on one of the flaps.

Take the box off your head and cut out the eye holes.

First draw circles.

Pierce a hole in the centre of each circle. Make cuts to the edge of the circle.

Perhaps you can write a little text on one flap: How to operate the robot.

Paint the mask with strong covering colours or use adhesive paper.

Introduce all robots to the group giving all the details:
Made in . . ., made by . . ., use, name, age . . .

Try it on once more to check if you can see through the holes.

Use very unusual colours.

Fix the bottle tops.

Find a name for your robot and write it on one of the flaps.

Turn the box upside down.

Think of a little text that your robot can say in English.

Ask your friend to mark the holes for the eyes with a pen or pencil.

Finally have a robot session in another class. They will like it.

Cut the circle out.

By the way:

Who did you show the experiments?
How did everybody like them?
Who liked which one best?
Who did not like which experiment?

4

Experiment D: Making your own clouds and a snowstorm

You need: a large tin, a small tin, ice or snow, cooking salt, a drinking straw; a torch, a magnifying glass, a pair of gloves.

Clouds are often floating ice drops or ice crystals. On a cold winter day you can watch clouds come from your mouth and condense into very small droplets. You can study this in an experiment.

Make yourself a small refrigerator (fridge) first.

Fill a large tin with a mixture of chopped or mashed ice or snow and cooking salt:

3 parts of ice or snow, 1 part of salt. Then put an empty small tin into the mixture.

In the smaller tin the air will cool off quickly.

Take your drinking straws and blow directly into the tin. Your breath will condense quickly into very small drops of water. The small drops will form a small cloud.

Shine your torch into the small tin and you will see the cloud more clearly.

Perhaps your chemistry or physics teacher has some solid carbon dioxide for you. Scratch a few tiny bits off this dry ice and let them fall into the tin. Be careful and wear gloves.

With your torch and a magnifying glass you will see thousands of tiny crystals. Blow into that crystal cloud and produce a snow storm.

Classroom discourse on experiments

I don't understand	how where why when	I you they	make . . . fix . . . add . . . put . . . connect . . . glue . . .

My problem is	I don't know how to . . .
	I can't fix . . .
	my . . . do not go together.
	my . . . slip(s) off.
	my . . . does/do not . . .
	the . . . break(s) . . .
	my . . . look(s) . . .

Again write a report by using the list below.

good sentence starters	sub-ject	verbs (past tense in reports)	the facts as the objects
At the beginning			
First		found	
Later		got	
Then	I	made myself/ourselves	
Next		filled	
After that		put	
Afterwards		took	
Now	we	blew	. . .
Finally		saw	. . .
In the end		shone	. . .
		got	. . .
		scratched	. . . .
		let	
		watched	
		blew	
		had	
		liked	

And then write short instructions

good sentence starters	sub-ject	verbs (in instructions simple form)	objects
At the beginning		find	. . .
First		get	. . .
Then		make yourself	. . .
And then	you	fill	. . .
Later		put	. . .
Next		take	. . .
After that		blow	. . .
Afterwards		can . . .	. . .
The next step is:		shine	. . .
Finally		get	. . .
		scratch	. . .
		let	. . .
		can	. . .
		blow	. . .
		produce	. . .

5

Experiment E: Burn a candle hollow

You need: a nail or a screw, a glass of water, a candle

Can you make a candle burn hollow?

Well, this is how the experiment goes.

Stick a nail or a screw into the bottom of a candle. Put the candle into a glass or a jam jar full of water. The candle will float with a few millimetres sticking out above the water.

Then light the candle.

Can you say what happened?

Show the hollow candle to friends.
Ask them how you can do such a thing.

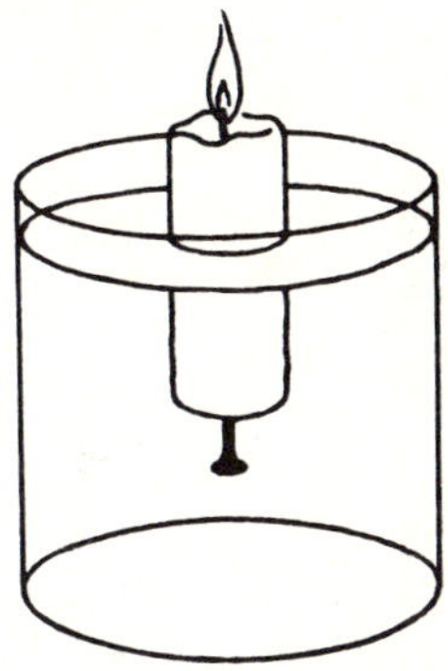

Put it in writing

good sentence starters	subject	verbs	objects
First	I it the wax	stuck put floated lighted burnt went was	. . . .

6

Experiment F: A waterproof bandage?

You will need: milk bottle, old nylon stocking, piece of gauze bandage, elastic band, water.

With the help of an elastic band fasten a piece of old nylon stocking across the mouth of a milk bottle.

Fill the bottle with water by holding it under a tap.

Of course, the water goes right through the nylon fabric.

When the bottle is full turn it upside down. What happens?

Then try the gauze bandage instead of the nylon.

What happens then?

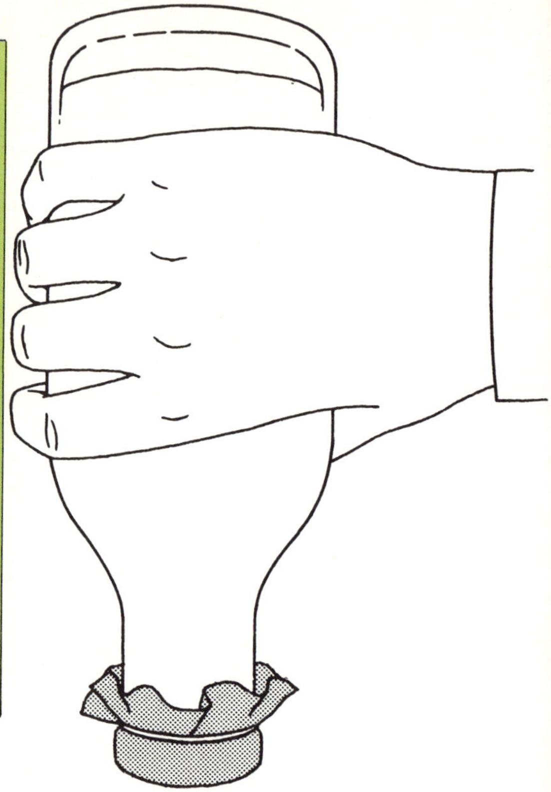

Experiment G: A miracle?

Light a small piece of candle and place it inside a glass. Wet a piece of cardboard with water, and put it on top of the glass. Then on top of this, mouth down, place another glass.

Lift one glass and the other comes as well.

Why?

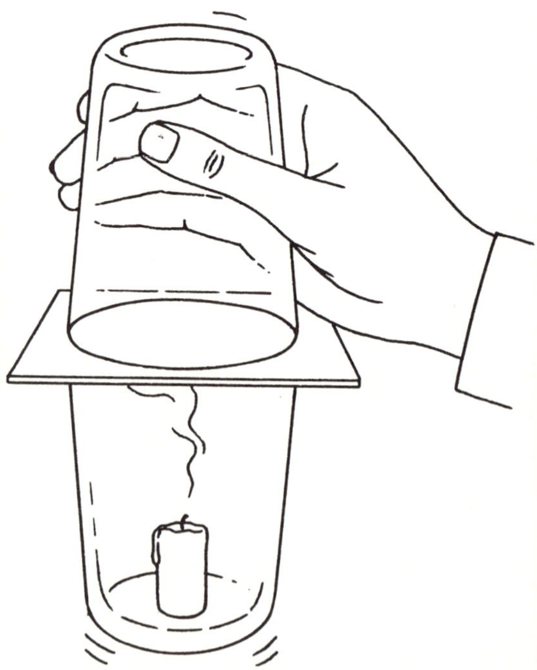

Describe your experiment and its results.

Preparing for visitors

By now you have learnt enough English to speak to foreigners, to help them find their way, to explain to them what life in Germany, in your town, in your school and in your family is like.
"Focus on Germany" helps you to get organized for a visiting group from abroad. The idea: make a list of facts, a guidebook.

Project 1

Focus on Germany

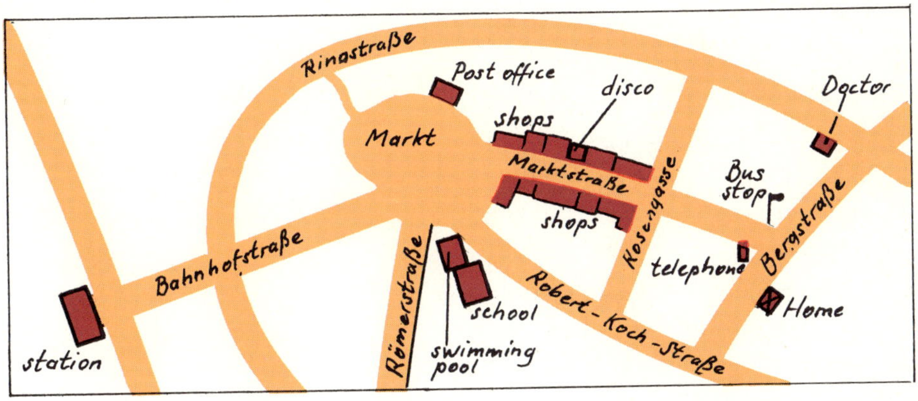

Firstly buy or draw a map of your place (town, village, suburb). Make dots where your school is and where the members of your group live. Use initials.

Secondly get or make photos of the most interesting places: disco, youth centre, pubs, sports-grounds and write something about them.

Thirdly find out and write down facts about places of interest for that particular group: street names, museums, places with names from their country.

Fourthly write down or copy English explanations about German money, postal rates for letters and postcards abroad, the telephone code and how to make telephone calls.

Fifthly make a list of means of transportation: buses, trains, coaches, and the costs of tickets.

Sixthly write down some German words and sentences with their English meanings, so that your friends can use them in shops etc.

Put the papers into a folder for each member of the group.

Focus on countries where English is spoken

Project 1

Focus on other countries

This sign in a shop means:
In this shop we speak English.
Or: In this shop English . . .

Information

More than 300 million people speak English as their first language. Millions of other people use English as a second language.

English as a native language is spoken in Great Britain, in Ireland, in the U.S.A., in Australia, Canada and New Zealand. English is used as a second language in a lot of countries in Asia and Africa: for example in India, in Sri Lanka, in Kenya, in Uganda, in Nigeria, in Malaysia, in Singapore.

Of course, English is understood in a lot of other countries, too. In Norway, Denmark, Sweden, Finland, Portugal, Thailand, Mexico, English is understood by most people and spoken by a lot of people.

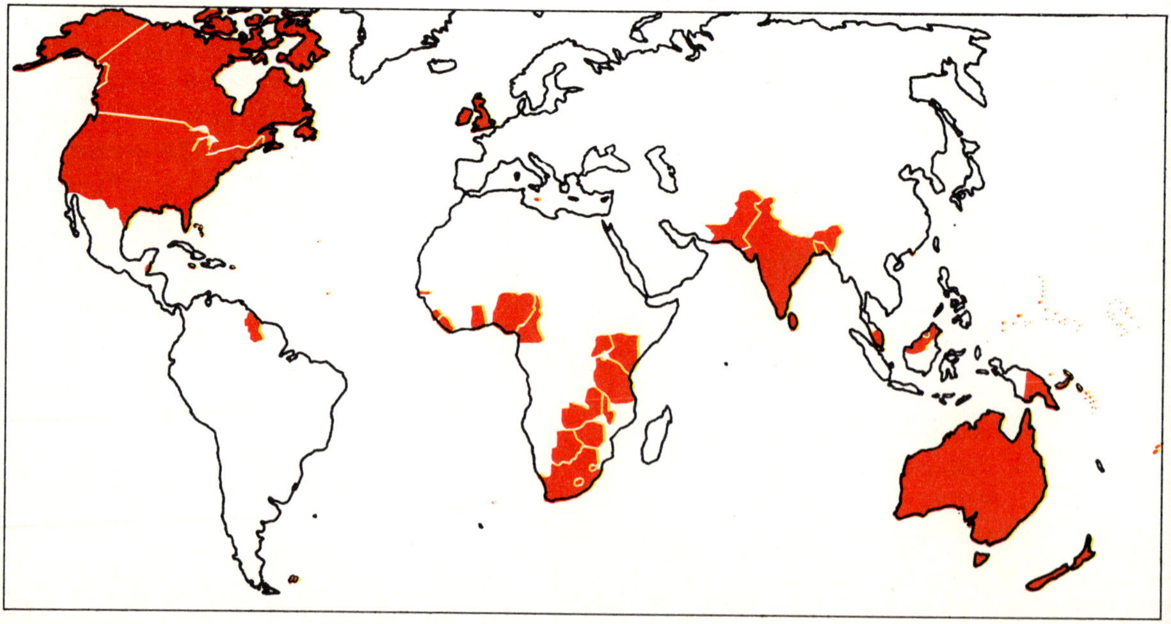

Languages of the World

There are over 3,000 languages spoken all over the world. Here are 13 languages spoken by over half the world's population:

Chinese	800–900 million people
English	350 million people
Spanish	250 million people
Hindi	190 million people
Russian	180 million people
Arabic	150 million people
Bengali	140 million people
Portuguese	110 million people
German	110 million people
Japanese	110 million people
French	85 million people
Malay	75 million people
Italian	65 million people
3,000 other languages	1,700 million people

Not in all the countries marked in the map English is spoken as the only or even the first language. In Canada, for example, 20% of the population speak only French, because a part of Canada was a French colony formerly. And did you know that not even in Great Britain English is the only language spoken? In Wales, for example, there are still many people who speak Welsh (a Gaelic language), and in Ireland you can hear Irish very often. Also in the USA there are many people, immigrants mostly, who speak Chinese, Italian, or Spanish as their first language.

Other countries use English as their oficial language, because they were British colonies formerly.

Task What countries? What languages?
Name the countries marked in the map and say what their native language is.
Your atlas may help you.
Listen to the tape.
Can you say which languages you hear?
What languages do your classmates speak?
How many words from other languages do you know?

Project 1

Language study package

MINI MODEL TEXT

Experiments are interesting and necessary. Without experiments you cannot learn anything in chemistry, physics and polytechnics. Cooking is not interesting without experiments. Even making friends is like an experiment. You try your best, but it may not work out or you find out you had the wrong ideas about it. I like experiments. That is why I like project one. And I am happy to try it in English.

We had great fun building **our dream castle.** We used cardboard, some glue, paper fasteners, a pen knife, a spool of thread, pins, some string and a board. Our castle was very big, but it nearly broke down. We built two high towers and a long main building with real chimneys. It looked funny, but we thought it was great. We got 25 points and came out second.

WORDS

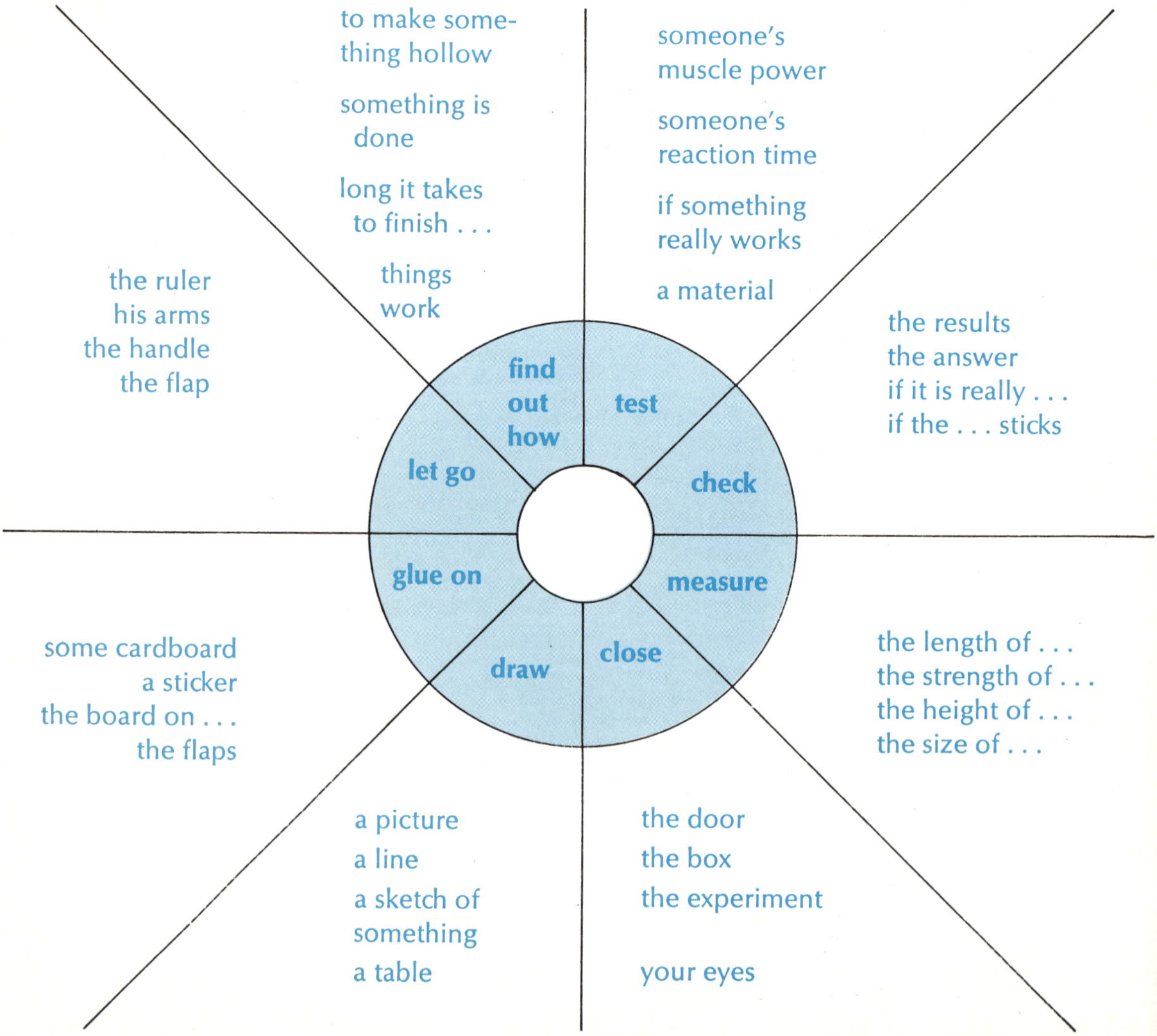

experiments			
verbs	**adverbs**	**adjectives**	**nouns**
make	suddenly	long	wood
produce	carefully	short	board
get	quickly	thick	metal
put	next	dry	paper
fix	then	wet	cardboard
place	afterwards	small	string
close	later	large	carton
prepare	finally	unusual	nail
find out how	together	empty	pin
test	directly	full	scotch tape
measure		hollow	glue
check			thread
hold			wire
tie			a pair of scissors
fasten			screwdriver
glue on			hammer
fill			flat pliers
empty			
let go			

Using adverbs

Fill in the missing adverbs.

. . .: Ralf is the fastest runner on the football team.
. . .: Come on. Fred runs . . . than Ralf.
. . .: No really. Ralf runs the . . . of all the football players. The coach said so.

. . .: Sandra is the slowest eater, I know.
. . .: Do you think so? You should eat lunch with Astrid sometimes. She eats even . . . than Sandra.

. . .: Boy, Peter was loud during math class this morning. I couldn't hear a word the teacher said.
. . .: You're right. Peter was really talking . . . And Annette was talking even . . . What was their problem?
. . .: They were talking about which pop group is the best . . .

With a partner plan a short dialogue like the ones above.

Adverbs of manner, place, and time

adverbs			
	manner	**place**	**time**
Experiment 3 went I finished the . . . I tried it out	beautifully quickly carefully	at home at my friend's in our garden	yesterday last night the day before yesterday
I tried it It worked out It did not come out	cautiously nicely well	in our kitchen in the classroom in my room	this morning on Monday last Sunday
	How?	**Where?**	**When?**

Adverb order (adverbs of manner, place and time)

Look at the following sentences. How many adverbs of manner are there? How many adverbs of place? How many adverbs of time?

1. My dog barks happily when she gets her food in the morning.
2. When the doorbell rings she hides in the kitchen.
3. In the evening we take a walk in the park together.
4. After that she hungrily races home.
5. She always waits for me to open the door for her.
6. She has never bitten anyone.
7. Sometimes she has fleas.
8. Then she has to take a bath in the bath tub.
9. We put her in a warm room afterwards,
10. and dry her with a large towel.
11. **Last winter she had been overrun by a car in the street.**
12. We took her to the vet as fast as we could.
13. She had to stay at the pet clinic for two weeks.
14. I was afraid that she would die.
15. But two days before Christmas we were allowed to fetch her home.
16. That was the happiest Christmas I ever had.

A reminder

the given fact	the result	
simple form or negation	can will 'll won't	+ simple form

Don't forget: 'll, won't, will

Make if-clauses

Begin the first sentence with 'if'. Connect the two sentences.
Put 'can' or 'will' or 'won't' in the second sentence.

You have a name for your robot.	→ suggestion what you can do	You write it on one of the flaps. (can)
You shine your torch into the tin.	→ result	You see the clouds more clearly. (will)
You blow into the crystal cloud.	→ result	You produce a snow storm. (can)
You don't understand why.	→ result	Your science teacher gives you an explanation. (can)
You turn the bottle upside down.	→ result	The water doesn't come out. (won't)
You lift one glass.	→ result	The other one comes as well. (will)
You don't like my robot.	→ suggestion	You make a better one. (Use can here.)

More if-clauses

If you . . . this experiment the candle . . . hollow. (make, burn)

If you . . . the strings a horizontal line you . . . a weightlifting champion. (make, be)

If your reaction time . . . poor you . . . a good race driver. (be, be not)

If you . . . a trip to Norway you . . . that most people there speak English quite well. (make, find out)

If you . . . in Ireland you . . . Gaelic a lot. (travel, hear)

If you . . . people in English they . . . in English probably. (address, answer)

If someone . . . English he . . . problems. (not speak, have)

If your visitor . . . German your English . . . him a lot. (not speak, help)

2 The Jeans stories

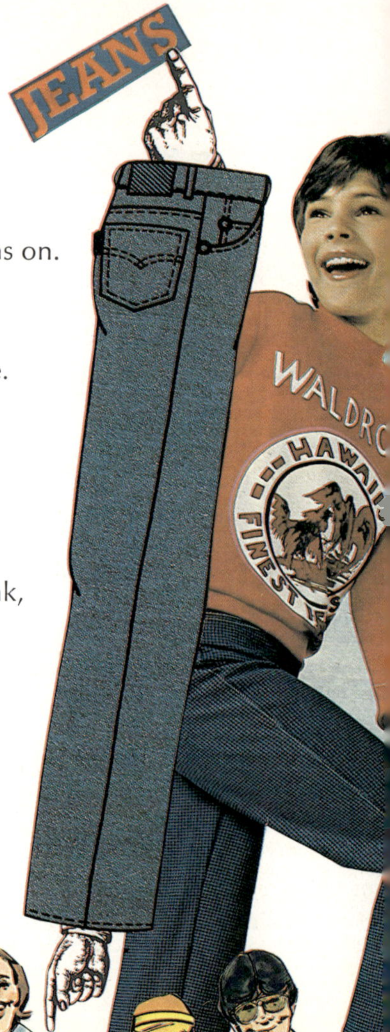

Project 2

Starters

Jeans on

When I wake up in the morning light
I put on my jeans and I feel all right.
I pull my blue jeans on, I pull my old blue jeans on.
I pull . . .

It's the weekend and I know that you're free,
so put on your jeans and come on out with me.
I need to have you near me,
I need to feel you close to me.
I need . . .

You and me we'll go motorbiking
in the sun and the wind and the rain.
I got money in my pocket, got a tiger in the tank,
and I'm king of the road again.

I meet you in the usual place,
I don't need a thing 'cept your pretty face
and I need to have your near me,
I need to feel you close to me.
I need . . .
I need . . .

You and me . . .

When I wake up . . .

David Dundas

A group of students in Giessen had this project:
"We tried to find out all about blue jeans for you. We collected all stories and songs about blue jeans. And we found a lot of different stories: commercials and stories about the history of a blue cloth called denim, or jeans, or dungaree, or indigo: (These words are French, Italian, English, Indian words.)
Here are some of the texts from our WORLD HISTORY OF JEANS STORIES."

French heels

All day long in my sloppy jeans
I just romp like a pup,
but at night I put my French heels on
and a teenage girl grows up.
All day long when my shirt-tail hangs
as I go round about,
but at night I put my French heels on
and a teenage girl steps out.
Hot road cars and trips to the shore are marvellous,
I suppose, but these years would be such a bore
without a chance to pose in dressed-up-clothes.
Growing up takes a lot of time
and I can't wait for the fun,
so at night I put my French heels on
and I pretend I'm twenty-one.

Debbie Reynolds

Which of the two songs do you like better?
Why?

Write 5 words from each song that go together well with jeans.

Get organized

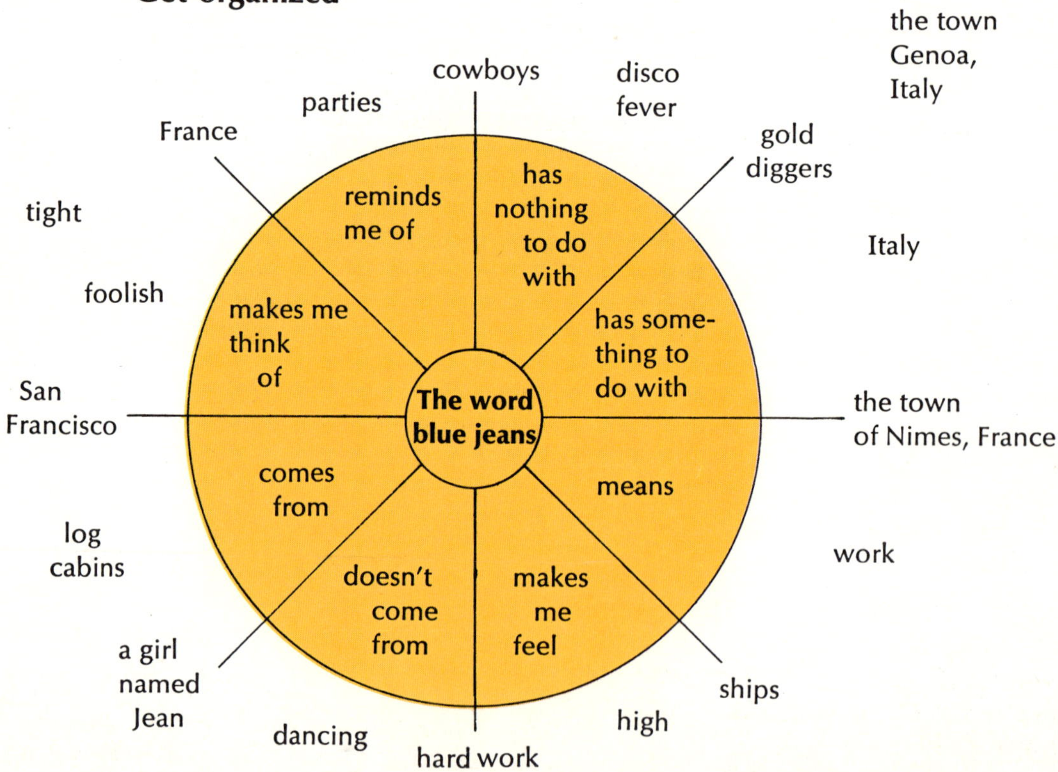

2

Divide into small groups and choose one of the following reading passages (A, B or C).

Project 2

The jeans stories

1 **A. Jeans**

We found this text in a Norwegian textbook for learning German.

Sie kennen doch Genua, die Stadt in Norditalien. Genua heißt auf Französisch Gênes. Wenn man das englisch ausspricht, dann klingt es wie „Jeans". Und darum heißen Jeans Jeans.

Um 1850 wohnte in San Francisco ein Mann mit dem Namen Levi Strauss. Er war ein Deutscher aus Bayern. Kalifornien war damals ein Goldgräberland. Levi Strauss ging davon aus, daß die Goldgräber Geld hatten. Er packte alle möglichen Waren auf einen Wagen und fuhr los. Er hatte recht. Man brauchte und kaufte seine Sachen.

Auch Segeltuch hatte er bei sich. Für Zelte, dachte er. Aber die Männer brauchten vor allem neue Hosen. Da ließ Levi Strauss Hosen nähen – Hosen aus Segeltuch. Die Idee war genial. Als sein Segeltuch alle war, kaufte er mehr, und bald waren „Levi's Hosen" bekannt. Sie waren genau das, was die Goldgräber brauchten.

Levi war damals 20 Jahre alt und hatte Mut und Ideen. Bald nahm er nicht mehr Segeltuch. Das war zu steif. Er kaufte festen Baumwollstoff für seine Hosen. Er tat noch etwas: Er färbte sie blau.

Unter den Goldgräbern waren Franzosen. Die wußten, daß die Matrosen aus Genua auch so blaue Hosen hatten. Genua – Gênes – Jeans: bald hießen Levi's Hosen „blue jeans".

Die Firma Levi Strauss existiert noch heute. Und wissen Sie, wie hoch der Umsatz ist? – Eine Milliarde Dollar im Jahr.

B. Levi Strauss

We compiled these facts from Levi Strauss texts.

In 1850, during the Gold Rush, a twenty-year-old immigrant from Bavaria named Levi Strauss stepped off the boat in San Francisco. He had with him a special cloth called 'Serge de Nimes' which was later called 'denim' in America. Levi Strauss hoped to sell the denim as material to make tents and covers for wagons, to the men who were going to the goldfields to look for gold.

"You should have brought pants to sell. In the goldfields we need strong pants that don't wear out", one young miner advised Strauss. So Levi Strauss took some of his denim to the nearest tailor and had him make the miner a pair of pants. The miner was so pleased with his pants that he told other miners about the wonderful new Levi's pants or 'Levis', and soon Levi Strauss had to open a shop, manufacturing enough trousers for the miners. The miners wanted trousers that were comfortable to ride in, that were low cut so they could bend over easily to pick up the gold from under their feet, and which had big useful pockets.

One miner complained that the gold in his pockets kept tearing them. So Levi put metal corners in the pockets to make them stronger. Very soon, miners and cowboys from all over came to get fitted up with Levi's pants.

Today, more than a hundred years later, Levi's pants walk round the world as 'Levi's blue jeans'.

C. Levi's pants

Levi Strauss sailed from Germany to New York in 1850. At that time, many people were travelling to California to look for gold. Levi decided to make his fortune, too. A friend told him to take some canvas with him. The miners wanted canvas for tents. Levi could sell the canvas and make a big profit. With the money he could buy tools to look for gold.

When Levi got off the ship in San Francisco, he told a friend about his plan. His friend laughed. "Why didn't you bring pants? I can't get a pair of pants that lasts more than two weeks!"

Levi took the canvas to a tailor. He made some pants. Then he sold the pants. Soon he was famous. Everybody wanted "Levi's Pants". Miners, farmers and cowboys needed strong Levis. They were always blue so that you could not see the dirt.

But why are "Levis" called "Jeans"? Well, Levi's wife was called Jean. In the beginning she helped him to make the pants.

Get organized

Compare the three texts.

Make up a list of what they say about Levi Strauss and write it in your exercise book.

	Text A	Text B	Text C
Levi came from			
He came to California in			
He lived in			
He was . . . (old)			
He sold			
He used to make			
people needed			
He asked			
The pants were called after			

Can you now write a text about "blue jeans: the true story"?

2 Task State your opinion

What's the reason for Strauss's big success?
Why did he get rich?
There is a formula for success in business:

Find a need and fill it.

L. Strauss found that people needed jeans.
Today's jeans producers think so, too.
Do you like or need jeans? Why? Why not?

Jeans make me feel fat and tight.

Jeans? Yes – But I like them pink!

Blue jeans are cheap.

Jeans have many pockets.

In blue jeans I feel happy and free.

Blue jeans are sexy.

Jeans go with everything.

All this blue jeans jazz is just propaganda – very clever propaganda.

Blue jeans are just practical.

I look much better in jeans than in other clothes.

I never wear jeans. They are awful: they look awful, they fit awfully, they smell awful.

Wearing blue jeans is like wearing a uniform.

In blue jeans we are all equal – rich and poor.

Jeans are "in".

Blue jeans bear hard wear without tear.

What jeans	make colour	do you prefer?

What other jeans clothes do you wear?

J . . . s
W . . . s

3 Why are jeans called jeans?

From the *Dictionary of Word and Phrase Origins* von William and Mary Morris, Harper & Row, New York 1962

"blue jeans"

In the West, especially among cattlemen, (cowboys)
they are usually called Levis.
In the East the name dungarees
is common, and everywhere your hear (in use)
jeans and denims.
Interestingly enough,
there is a story behind each of these names –
and it's hard to tell
which of the four is more unusual.

Take jeans, for example.
Although thousands of girls
named Jean have worn them
there is no connection at all (they have nothing to do with each other)
between the girl's name
and the name of the garment. (piece of clothing)
It's actually an altered form of "Genoa",
where the cloth was once woven.

Similarly, denim comes from the phrase
serge de Nimes,
after the city of Nimes, France.

Dungaree is the most exotic of the names,
though. It comes to us all the way
from fabled Hindustan,
where the word dungri was used
for a coarsely woven fabric (roughly)
for tents and sails.
After a while sailors made up
work clothes from the material
and so dungarees were invented.

Levis, of course, are American.
The name comes from Levi Strauss,
a San Francisco clothing merchant
of the Gold Rush days.
(person who sells clothes)

Levi Strauss

Note-making I

In this book you will practise five ways of note-making. Here is the first one: the main-point-method. In the text above the main points are the four names for jeans. Write them down. Then shut your book and try to remember where these names came from. Write a short paragraph.

4 Have you got your facts right?

Which of these sentences are false?

1 Levi Strauss invented the blue jeans in 1850.

2 Denim canvas was first made in France.

3 Dungaree is the English spelling of the Hindi word DUNGRI.

4 Levi Strauss' invention were the rivets on the corners of pockets.

5 Levi's first trousers were mostly sold to gold miners.

6 The miners put the gold ore into their pockets.

7 Levi's wife was called Jean and she had blue jeans. That's why the trousers are called blue jeans.

8 The pocket rivets are made of gold.

9 Levi Strauss added paper clips to the trousers.

10 Denim is a name for cotton cloth.

11 Miners loaded their pockets with dollars.

12 The Gold Rush to California began in 1849.

13 Most German emigrants left Germany for America because of the gold in California.

2

Project 2

Focus on Germany

Hints for things

to do and say on the first day

- Let me show you the main parts of X.
- We might go to the Tourist Information Office and get a street map of X.
- I could show you where my mother and my father work.
- I could take you to a place from where you have a good view of the area.
- Would you like to see or do something special?
- I'll show you the post office and the bus stop where you catch the bus to . . .
- I might show you some old . . .
- I could take you to . . .
- Have you ever been inside a . . .?
- Are you interested in sports events?
- We could go to the football match on . . . or to the . . . on . . .
- What else would you like to do?

Eating and drinking

Some foreigners think that Germans live on sauerkraut, schnitzel, liversausage and beer.
Most foreigners believe that too many Germans are too fat.
First there are the kiosks, stands and snack bars where you buy soft drinks and beer and which offer all kinds of hot dog, fried chicken and potato salad.
These places (the word is IMBISS) are usually quite cheap and mostly clean.
In most towns and cities you have the usual Whimpy or McDonald restaurants that are very popular among teenagers.
In most fish shops in city centres you get excellent fish and chips and other meals at reasonable prices.

Crisp cheese, ham, fish or chicken rolls are sold in most snack bars, kiosks and fish shops. Some butchers sell them, too.
German bread (brown bread) can be a delicacy. There are hundreds of sorts.
Germans eat a lot of bread.
If you go in for sweets the department stores are your places to go to.
But there are other sweet shops, too, often belonging to a chain of shops.
In the last ten years a lot of Greek, Italian, Chinese, Turkish, Balkan, French, Vietnamese and other restaurants have been opened. Some of them are not only excellent, but also reasonably cheap.
To many Germans pizzas are the most delicious quick meals.

2

Project 2

Focus on other countries

Scotland

As you quite certainly know Great Britain consists of three parts: England, Wales, and Scotland. Here we want to talk about Scotland.

When you think of Scotland, you certainly have these pictures in mind:

old castles

kilts and bagpipes

"Lochs", the Scottish lakes

sheep grazing on green meadows

Some facts:

size: 78 775 sq.km
capital: Edinburgh
population: 5 180 000 (approximately)

Scotland is part of the United Kingdom of Great Britain and Northern Ireland.

But did you also know that

- Scotland has not always been part of the United Kingdom, but had fought violently against England for hundreds of years, until it finally came under English rule in 1603.
- during the industrial revolution coal mining, ship building and the production of steel and other metals developed in Scotland, especially in Clydeside, Glasgow and Dundee;
- the Scots have their own church and even their own banknotes;
- Great Britain has enough North Sea oil off the shores of Scotland to be independent from oil imports?

Map of the Scottish oil fields

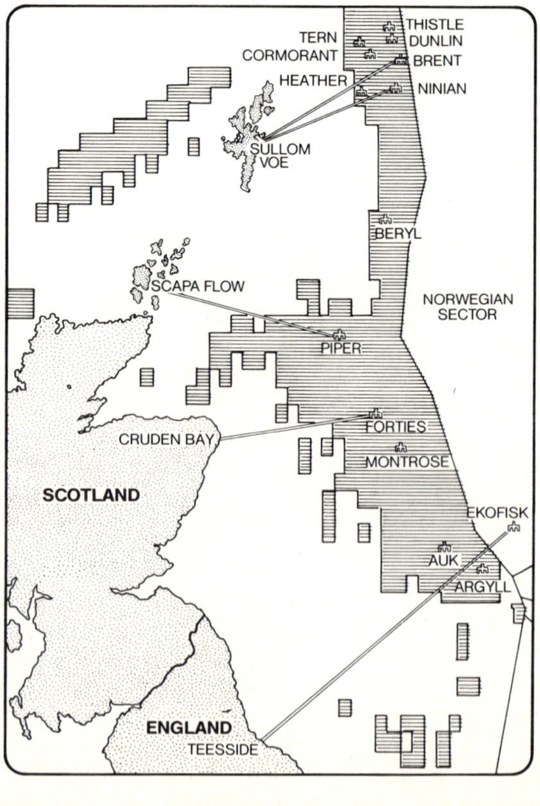

2

Project 2

Language study package

MINI MODEL TEXT

I think **bluejeans** are both practical and good-looking. They are not very expensive, they fit everybody because there are so many sizes. You can wear jeans with everything. In bluejeans you feel free and flexible. They have a lot of pockets. There are many kinds of jeans, carrot jeans, striped jeans, dark or light bluejeans etc. Some jeans are terribly expensive. There are jeans shops all over Germany. They sell shirts, blouses, sweaters, jumpers, socks, stockings, coats, too. They spend a lot of money on ads.

WORDS

I	never always usually don't like to	wear make buy like own love wash iron	my jeans cheap jeans expensive jeans tight jeans	in . . . shops every day when I go to school when I go to the disco when I go to the church when I go to my grandmother's birthday party

Clothes Rolls Jeans All people A boxer My clothes	should be	tight. equal. strong. crisp. comfortable. inexpensive.

Write at least twelve pairs of sentences.
In the first sentence of each pair write what you do.
In the second sentence explain why.

You might join the two sentences by using **therefore, for, because.**

Example: I like my jeans. They are comfortable.
Or: I like my jeans because they are comfortable.

Using language to talk about the past

A	B
After he had left Bavaria	he migrated to America.
When he had landed in California	he opened a shop.
He had never made trousers	before he came to California.
When he had been there a few years	he became rich.
When they had put rivets on the corners	the pockets didn't tear easily.
Whenever they had found a piece of ore	they put it in their pockets.

Das PAST in diesen Sätzen zeigt, daß das Ereignis B in der Vergangenheit vollendet wurde. Das PAST PERFECT zeigt, daß das Ereignis A vor dem Ereignis B stattfand.

PAST PERFECT = had + past participle

The PAST in these sentences shows that event B was completed in the past. The PAST PERFECT shows that event A took place before event B.

past time (= the time before now)

PAST PERFECT (A)	PAST (B)
After we had left New York,	we met lots of nice people.
We had read about Sacramento.	We wanted to visit it.

More past practice

Write 7 sentences about what you did during your summer holidays.

Example After I had gone camping I visited my grandparents.

Language material

go swimming	visit my grandparents	because
go to the seashore	read a lot of books	when
go sightseeing	ride my bicycle	after
go camping	be sick	before
go to the mountains	have a job	
visit my friends	work as a . . .	

Talking about events in the past: past progressive

1. John **was cleaning** his tennis shoes at 11:00 a.m.
   (John had started cleaning his shoes before 11:00 a.m.
   and he continued cleaning after that time.)
2. John **was cleaning** his tennis shoes when the telephone rang.
   (John had started cleaning his shoes before the telephone rang.)
3. John **was cleaning** his tennis shoes while his brother **was reading** a book.
   (These two events were going on at the same time.)

Note:
When you describe how several past events fit together you use the past progressive.

past progressive = past form of BE (was/were) + -ing form

The past progressive usually expresses

1. that an event in the past was not yet complete at a certain moment (sentence 1);
2. that an event was not yet complete when another event happened (sentence 2);
3. that two events were going on at the same time (sentence 3).

Talking about events in the past: practice

Practice Put the verbs in parentheses into the past progressive.

Elizabeth (read) the instructions while Kurt (fetch) a thick book.
Walter (fix) the antenna when it (break) off in his hand.
While Sylvia (try on) the robot mask Sandra (laugh) at her.
Levi Strauss (sail) to San Francisco when people (look) for gold in California.

Soon after 1850 he (make) pants.
Today people (wear) jeans all over the world.
While Volker (work) a miracle someone took his matches away.
Birgit (fool) a strong weight-lifter while Jan (test) Walter's reaction time.

Simple past – past progressive

simple past		past progressive	
time in the past	event (complete)	time in the past	event (going on)
Yesterday	John **cleaned** his tennis shoes.	At 11 a.m.	John **was cleaning** his shoes.
		When the telephone **rang**	John **was cleaning** his shoes.
		While his brother **was reading** a book	John **was cleaning** his shoes.
At a definite time in the past the event was complete.		At a definite time in the past the event was going on.	

Tall tales

Tall tales are lies that make people laugh. In this exercise you will practise using the simple past and the past progressive by telling tall tales.

Practice On a piece of paper write at least 5 tall tales about things you did yesterday, last week, last month, etc.

Examples Last week I ran to Paris and back.
Last month I counted 35 elephants in my garden.

Then trade papers with a partner and use his tales to write at least 5 even taller tales.

Examples While you were counting 35 elephants, I was baking 35 cakes.
While you were running to Paris and back, I was jumping over the Empire State Building.

Events in the past: practice

Put the verbs in parentheses into the simple past or the past progressive.

. . .: When (make) you these cookies?
. . .: I (bake) them yesterday afternoon. Why?
. . .: They taste two weeks old.

▶
. . .: What (do) you last night at 8:00? I (try) to call you.
. . .: I (wash) my hair. I didn't hear the phone.

Tenses
A reminder

<table>
<tr><th>tenses</th><th>past time</th><th>present time</th><th>future time</th></tr>
<tr><td>present</td><td></td><td>Bill likes music.</td><td></td></tr>
<tr><td>present perfect</td><td colspan="2">He has lived there since 1975</td><td></td></tr>
<tr><td>past</td><td>His sister lived there until 1976</td><td></td><td></td></tr>
<tr><td>past perfect</td><td>She had lived in Kentucky before she moved to Vermont</td><td></td><td></td></tr>
<tr><td>future</td><td></td><td></td><td>He will start college in one year</td></tr>
</table>

Use this table to explain to a partner when the different tenses are used.

Fill in the correct verb forms

American travellers in Germany . . . . . remember that the stores . . . . . closed in the evenings.	(must, be)
In France many stores . . . . . open in the evenings.	(be)
Eight years ago Americans . . . . . 4 marks for every dollar. Now they . . . . . about 2 marks.	(get)
After airplane tickets across the Atlantic . . . . . cheaper in the 1970's, many more people . . . . . travel between the USA and Europe.	(become) (can)
When you . . . . . at Frankfurt airport tomorrow morning, you . . . . . probably . . . . . very tired.	(arrive, feel)
Many American tourists . . . . . never . . . . . with a German before their trip to Europe.	(talk)
For this reason, they . . . . . very happy when someone . . . . . to them on a train or in a restaurant.	(be) (speak)
Several years ago I . . . . . two German tourists in my hometown in the USA. They . . . . their street map a few minutes before and . . . . . not . . . . . where their hotel was.	(meet) (lose, know)
I . . . . . them find their way and we . . . . . a long talk about Germans and Americans.	(help, have)

3 Indians

Project 3

Starters

Indians hunting buffaloes

Apache women moving camp

Battle of the Big Horn

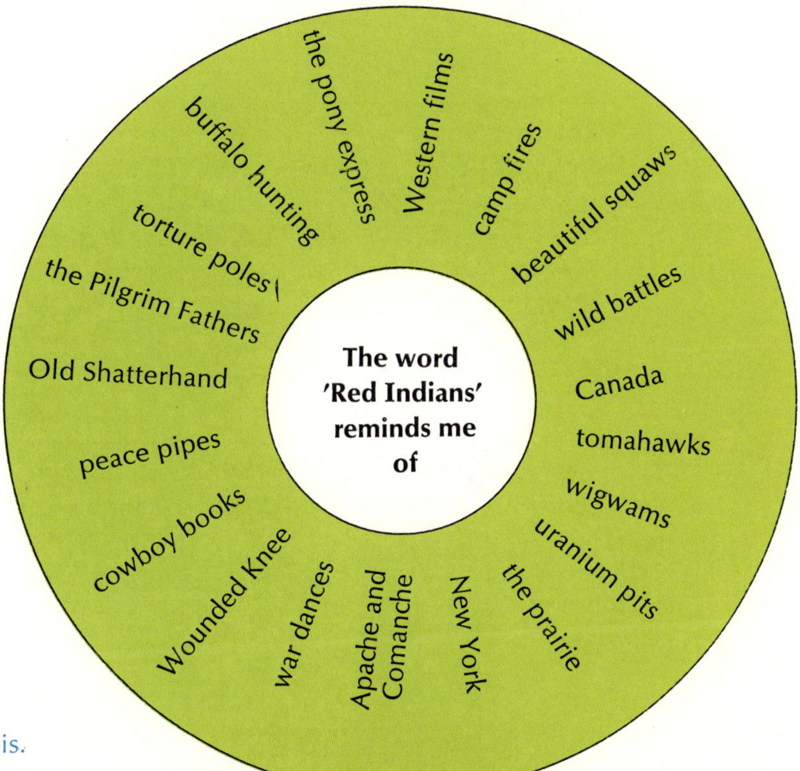

I've no idea what . . . | is.
are.

Wo nur die Macht zählt

Wo Colorado, Utah, Arizona und Neu-Mexico aneinanderstoßen, liegt die Hochebene von Colorado. Hier wurden viele Indianer zurückgelassen oder besser gesagt: zurückgestoßen. Heute ist dieses Land zum Schauplatz eines Dramas geworden. „National specified area" nennen es die Behörden, was soviel heißen soll wie: Diese Region muß den nationalen Interessen zum Opfer gebracht werden. Hier nämlich liegt annähernd die Hälfte der amerikanischen Uran-Reserven, liegen zwei Drittel der Ölschiefer-Vorkommen und reiche Lagerstätten an Kohle, deren Umfang noch nicht einmal abgegrenzt worden ist.

Die Indianer wissen schon, weshalb sie von einer Zone des „nationalen Desasters" sprechen. Mehr als 99 Prozent der in dem radiumhaltigen Gestein vorkommenden Radioaktivität nämlich verbleiben an Ort und Stelle – im Abraum. Und auf der Hochebene von Colorado ist mehr Strahlung konzentriert als auf dem gesamten übrigen Territorium der Vereinigten Staaten zusammengenommen.

Was aber noch schlimmer ist: Die Hauptmasse des Abraums aus der Urangewinnung ist niemals gesichert worden. Das ausgemahlene Gestein wird in die Flüsse gekippt und schließlich von den reißenden Gewässern talwärts geführt, den Colorado hinab. Aber auch Wind und Regen wirken an der gründlichen Verteilung des radioaktiven Abfalls mit.

So kommt es immer häufiger zu Todesfällen. Immer mehr Uranarbeiter sterben. Und ihre Witwen wissen, daß der schleichende Tod auch nach ihnen und ihren Kindern greift.

Uranium is necessary for nuclear power. It was found in an area where Colorado, Utah, Arizona and New Mexico meet. The government called this area a "national specified area". The area was Indian country. The rivers are polluted. Mount Taylor, the sacred mountain of Navajos and Pueblos, was turned into a uranium pit. Water and the air are radio active. A lot of workers have died. Indians fight for their right to live and to live in the way they like.

Task

Compare the German with the English passage.
Shut your book and write down in English what you remember.

William Spotted Horse

Hi! My name is William Spotted Horse.

I was born on the Pine Ridge Reservation in North Dakota. I lived there together with my family and my tribe.

One day – I was only 5 years old – a big yellow bus came to our reservation. All of us kids were just picked up and taken away to a boarding school.

I did not like that boarding school at all, because it was so different from our way of life. There were no Indian teachers and we couldn't understand the white man's language when we came there. We did not know any English. The school was also far away from home – 100 miles! – and we couldn't see our parents.

That's why I dropped out of the school after the 5th grade. I went back to our reservation afterwards.

But life on the reservation was very depressing: the living conditions were very poor. There was no job for me and there was no money, too. Many of our young people took drugs, many others drank too much alcohol, some even committed suicide.

I also felt sad about such bad conditions. And I felt bored, because: what was there to do on the reservation?

I wanted to get away from it soon!

That's why I moved to San Francisco in 1955. Now I was in one of the white man's big cities with its industry, skyscrapers, cinemas, theatres and city-lights!

I looked for a job – but it was difficult for me to get one: I was untrained for most jobs.

And I was completely unprepared for the modern American way of life. I came from the country and did not know anything about computers, traffic, shopping-centers and all these things! And most of all: I felt very lonely and homesick in the white man's world. I missed my tribe and my family. I was used to live in a large group.

That's why I left San Francisco and its exciting life behind and I went back to the country, to my people on the reservation.

That was in 1956 . . .

Note-making II. the verb method

Take notes about what Spotted Horse did; that is: take the verb from each sentence and write it down. (If there is another important word going with the verb take it, too.)

1. At the reservation: born – lived there – bus came – . . .
2. At school: . . .
3. At the reservation
4. At San Francisco
5. At . . .

How might Spotted Horse's story go on?

3

Project 3

The old West

The Indians of North America

1 Where did the Indians live?

Task Using the map above and a topographical map of North America locate each of the following tribes.

1. Iroquois
2. Seminole
3. Nez Perce
4. Cherokee
5. Paiute
6. Comanche

The . . . lived in . . . They were . . .

State:

a) the general geographical location of the tribe

b) the important geographical features near which the tribe lived, for example:
a river
a lake
a mountain range
a desert
plains
an ocean

c) the present states in which each tribe lived.

Ask your classmates to locate other tribes.

❷ The first Americans

The first Americans came in the North American continent from Siberia, probably crossing a land bridge over the Bering Strait. They moved south through Alaska and spread throughout North and South America.

We seldom stop to think that our name for the first Americans – Indians – has no real meaning for the people who call themselves Cherokee, Sioux, or Hopi.

Just as each tribe has its own name, it also has its own way of life, beliefs, and language.

When Christopher Columbus landed in the Bahamas he called the people there Indians because he thought he had reached India.

The Sioux

"The whites were always trying to make the Indians give up their life and live like white men – go to farming, work hard and do as they did – and the Indians did not know how to do that, and did not want to anyway . . ."

Wamditanka (Big Eagle) of the Santee Sioux

The horse and the buffalo were the two most important factors in the life of the Plains Sioux. The Spanish brought the first horses to the Americans in the 16th century. Indians throughout midwestern North America soon started hunting the buffalo on horseback. A lot of Sioux bands left their permanent farms on the edge of the Great Plains to become nomads, following the buffalo herds across the nothern Plains. One hunter on horseback could shoot enough buffalo in one day to feed his family for a year. The buffalo provided the Sioux with more than just food. From the buffalo came clothing, tepee covers, pots, ropes and warm blankets. Horns, hoofs, and bones were made into tools, weapons and glue. Because of the buffalo and the horse the Plains Sioux had enough food, shelter or clothing.

Plains Sioux chiefs were chosen because of special courage or wisdom, but they only gave advice, not orders. A council of older men made decisions for the band.

Once a year in summer the Plains Sioux had their most important religious ceremony, the Sun Dance. During this ceremony they danced and went without food or water for days in return for help from their gods.

Task Make notes about the following main points: government, religion and food-getting. Give a short talk about the Sioux.
Perhaps you have books about other Indian tribes.
You might choose one tribe, make notes from your book and give a short talk in class.

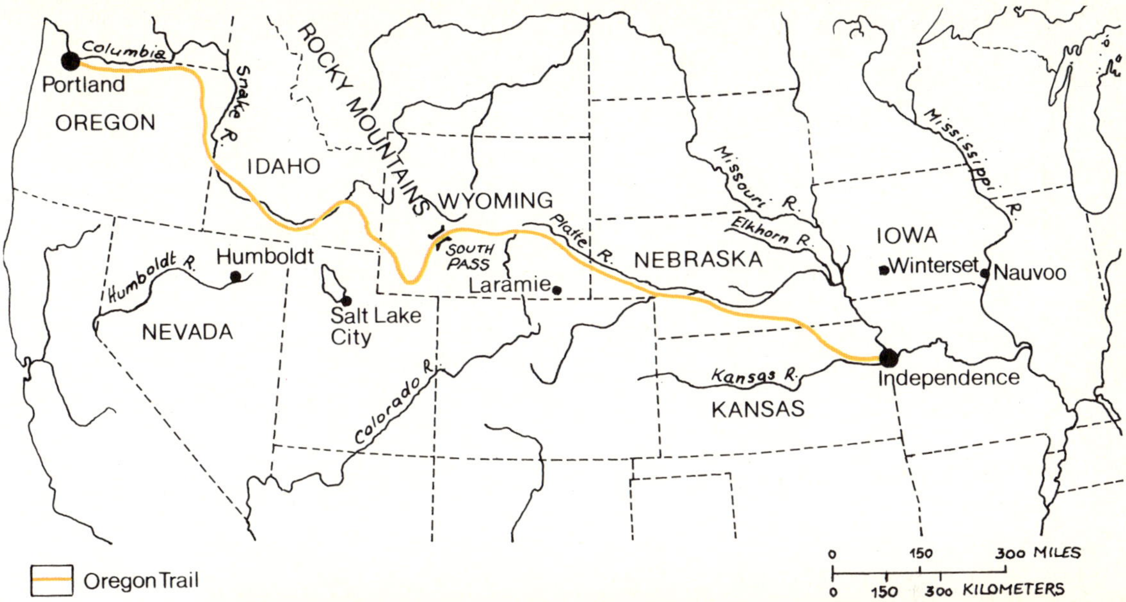

3

The Oregon Trail – a trail through Indian country

Oregon Trail, overland emigrants trail from Missouri to Columbia.

The towns Independence and Westport (now in Kansas City) were the favourite starting points. The first emigrants trail was led by John Bidwell in 1841. The first trail to reach Oregon was led by Elijah White in 1842.

Look at the map above and answer the following questions about the Oregon Trail.

1. Which present day states did the pioneers travel through?
2. How many rivers did the pioneers have to cross on their way to Oregon? Which ones?
3. What is the longest distance between rivers that the pioneers had to cross?
4. In order to reach Oregon before the winter snows, the pioneers had to travel an average of 20–25 miles per day. Why did many turn back after 50–55 days? What lay before them?
5. What difference in altitude did the pioneers experience on their journey?
6. For many years after 1846, the second half of the Oregon Trail was littered with furniture, china and other household goods. Why?
7. Compare a trip through Europe to the trek the Oregon pioneers made. Take Frankfurt as the starting point and find a destination that is as far away as Oregon from St. Louis.

People on the Oregon Trail

Simon Goodacre

Simon Goodacre was a Presbyterian
minister from a small town in Pennsylvania,
who was going to take over a church
in Oregon.

He was 51 years old
and he had a wife and seven children.
His oldest child was 15.

Goodacre was a very calm and friendly
man.
He was well-educated.

He had gone to Princeton University.

There were other men on the wagon train
who – like Goodacre – could read and
write.

Nathan Young

Nathan Young was a 25 year old farmer,
travelling to Oregon with his younger
brother, Henry, who was 19.

As a young boy
Young had helped his parents
start a farm in Iowa,
which had become quite successful.
All his life he had lived
near the wilderness
and he was used to working hard.

For Young and his brother,
the trek to Oregon
was an exciting adventure.

Kendall Stewart

Kendall Stewart, 35, was also a farmer,
but he and his family came from Missouri.
Stewart had a wife,
who was expecting a baby,
and three sons.
The Stewarts' farm in Missouri
had been too small
for the growing family.
Stewart was a man
full of energy
and a tough worker.
He was also a very helpful man
liked by his neighbours.
But he was also a bit hot-tempered
and knew well
how to use his fists in a fight.

Taylor Potts

Taylor Potts had left his tobacco farm
in Kentucky with his wife and six children.
His rich neighbours had used slaves
to do the hard work for them. He
had done all the work himself,
and he had not produced enough tobacco
to make a living. Potts was 37 years old.
He was a careful man
who did not decide things quickly.
Like most of the men in the trek
he dreamed of a better,
more secure and successful life
for his family in Oregon.

Task: Make a list of the four men

name	Simon Goodacre	**job**	
age		**reason for being in the trek**	
from			
character		**hopes/plans/ dreams**	
family			

Choosing a wagon master

The wagon master or pilot of the wagon train was usually one of the pioneers elected by the others after the first days of the trek.
He had to plan the daily route of the trek, he had to organize working teams, and he had to choose the resting places. There was a guide (scout), too, but the wagon master was responsible for the trek.

Task Look at the text about people on the Oregon Trail.
Which of them would you choose as wagon master?
Which of your classmates would you elect as pilot?

A wagon master had to be/ didn't have to be …

young, religious, well educated, hot-tempered, a man, careful, a good leader, a hard worker, successful, rich, diplomatic, humorous, strict, tough, calm, friendly, old, a good politician, helpful, strong, a perfect scout, a good shot

Language aids

I agree. – I don't think so.	Why didn't they choose …
A leader needn't be …,	I think … did not have to be …
but he must be …	I believe … had to be …

4 The Sioux – A timeline

until ca. 1650	Sioux tribes live in villages on the edge of great plains and are semi-nomadic farmers. They hunt buffalo on foot.
1540	Sioux make first contacts with Whites, Spanish explorers in present state of Kansas.
1540–1700	Spanish bring horses into North America. The use of horses spreads slowly northward through the Plains.
1650–1800	Bands of Sioux migrate westward on to the Plains.
ca. 1740	Most Sioux use horses and live as nomadic buffalo hunters on the Plains.
ca. 1790	The Sioux have begun to use guns.
1840–1850	Settlers and miners on their way to Oregon and California travel through Sioux land. The Sioux attack and kill many invaders. The U.S. government builds forts along the Oregon Trail to protect settlers.
1850–1868	The U.S. government wages war on the Sioux. There are large and bloody battles throughout the Northern Plains.
1868	A treaty is signed with the Sioux which gives them a huge reservation including the Black Hills. Settlers and miners break the treaty immediately by settling in the reservation.
1874	Gold is discovered in the Black Hills.
1876	Thousands of miners enter the reservation. The Sioux try to defend their land. Total war breaks out again. General George Custer and soldiers are killed in a large battle at Little Big Horn.
1877–1881	One by one all the Sioux bands are defeated.
1889	A new treaty is made and the Sioux reservation is cut in half and divided into 5 separate sections.
1890	153 Sioux men, women, and children are killed at Wounded Knee, South Dakota.
	The Sioux are finally and totally defeated.

Task Can you say and write all this in the past form?

Background information

In 1889 the government took away nearly half of their land because gold had been discovered in the Black Hills.
In that same year a very dry summer destroyed all their crops and the government started sending them less food.
In the following 2 winters many of the Sioux starved and a measles epidemic killed hundreds of their children who were weak from hunger.

In their desperation the Sioux began stealing cattle and planning revolt.
Their revolt was supported by a new religious ceremony called the "Ghost Dance".

Believers thought that those who danced the "Ghost Dance"

and wore "Ghost Shirts" could not be killed.
They also believed that the Whites would soon disappear from the Plains and the Sioux could return to their old ways.

The government outlawed the "Ghost Dance" and arrested the leaders who taught it.
Soldiers on the reservations were ordered to collect all the Indians' guns.

Big Foot's band was one of the last bands to follow these orders.

Task Complete the short sentences in the table by putting in words above and under the verbs.

When?/Why?	In 1889	after			and
Who? or What?	the US government				the Sioux
VERBS	took away	had been discovered	destroyed	sent	were
					desperate

When?/Why?			because	later	also
Who? or What?					
VERBS	starved	killed	were	began	were planning
	terribly				

5 The battle of Wounded Knee

Choose one of the following texts for reading (A, B, or C).

A.

"All the News That's Fit to Print"

The New York Times

CITY EDITION

Metropolitan area weather: Periods of light snow or flurries today, tonight. Temperature range: today 25-30; yesterday 25-31. Details are on page A18.

What Happened at Wounded Knee?

A Fight with the Big Foot's Band Causes a Battle

Tuesday, December 30, 1890

... Big Foot's Band, numbering 150 warriors, surrendered yesterday to Major Whiteside and the Seventh Cavalry. They were taken to the old camp on Wounded Knee Creek. This morning the Indians were ordered to come forward from the tents. This was done, the squaws and children remaining behind the tepees.

The warriors moved a short distance from the camp. The Indians were ordered to give up their guns but they only produced two. A small group of soldiers began to search the village and found 38 guns, although the squaws tried to hide them.

During the search the warriors began to move. All of a sudden they threw their hands to the ground and began firing at the troops. The soldiers began shooting after the Indians had fired at least fifty shots. They aimed at the warriors but some women and children were killed in the confusion. The warriors ran back to their tepees. Some of them continued firing from among their woman and children. The warriors, women and children then ran together to the south. The soldiers fired at them as they ran. Many of the Indians tried to hide in a ravine. They were shot down wherever found. Soldiers on horses pursued the redskins who tried to escape from the ravine and few of the band were alive at the end of the battle.

The members of the Seventh Cavalry have once more shown themselves to be heroes in deeds of daring. The Indians were not all armed with guns, many of them having only knives and clubs.

B.

The New York Times February 12, 1891

Indians tell their story

The Sioux Indian conference ended
in Washington today.
The feature of today's meeting was topic
the story of the fight at Wounded Knee,
which was told by Turning Hawk
and American Horse.

Turning Hawk: Our people were taken
to Wounded Knee Creek.
The soldiers demanded their guns. asked for
When the men had given them up,
they were taken away from their families,
from their tepees to a certain spot. place
There was a crazy young man,
who fired his gun.
Immediately the soldiers fired back
and began killing everyone.

American Horse: All the men
who were standing around the man
who fired the first shot
were killed there.
Those who escaped the first shots got away
got into the ravine. narrow place between hills
They were followed on both sides
by some of the soldiers
and were shot down.

Then other soldiers turned their guns
on the women and children
who were in the tepees. tents
They fled in two directions,
separate from the men. not with
The soldiers followed
and killed most of them.

After most of them had been killed,
a cry was made
that everyone should come out
and they would be safe.
Little boys who were not wounded
came out of their hiding places.
As soon as they came in sight,
several soldiers surrounded and killed them. went around them

C.

Another version

White lance:

They called for guns and arms,
so all of us gave the guns
and they were stacked up
in the center.

Dog Chief:

They would go right into the tents
and come out with bundles
and tear them open.
They brought our axes,
knives, and tent stakes
and piled them near the guns.

Loise Weasel Bear:

We tried to run,
but they shot us
like we were a buffalo.
I know there are some good white people,
but the soldiers must be mean
to shoot children and women.
Indian soldiers would not do that
to white children.

Get organized

Try to answer the following questions about the events at Wounded Knee.

According to your document:

1. What did the Indians do with their guns?
2. Did the Indians give up their guns **willingly?**
3. **Who** fired the first shot?
4. **How many shots** were fired before the other side shot back?
5. Did **the warriors flee in the same direction** as the women and children or did they **flee in another** direction?
6. Did the soldiers **shoot the women and children on purpose** or **by accident?**
7. Was anybody killed?

A speaker for each group should read his group's answers to the questions.
Collect the answers in note form on the blackboard or on an overhead transparency.
Use a table like below.
If you write the answers down in whole sentences you will have a summary of the events at Wounded Knee.

Comparing notes

	document A	document B	document C
1.			
2.			
3.			
...			

3

Project 3

Focus on Germany

Public holidays in Germany

The following public holidays are observed throughout the Federal Republic of Germany:

New Year's Day	January 1
Good Friday	Friday before Easter
Easter Monday	Monday following Easter Sunday
Labour Day	May 1
Ascension Day	Ten days before Whit Sunday
Whit Monday	Monday following Whit Sunday
National public holiday	June 17
Christmas Eve	December 24 (only the afternoon)
Christmas Day	December 25
Boxing Day	December 26
New Year's Eve	January 31 (only the afternoon)

Most of the public holidays in the Federal Republic of Germany are of religious origin. So there are some which are celebrated only in the Catholic or only in the Protestant areas. The following public holidays are observed in only some of the Federal „Länder":

Epiphany	January 6
Rose Monday	Seven weeks before Easter Monday
Shrove Tuesday	The day following Rose Monday (These two days form the peak of the carnival season in the appropriate areas).
Corpus Christi	The second Thursday after Whitsun
Assumption Day	August 15
All Saints Day	November 1
Day of Prayer and Repentence	The third Wednesday in November

Shopping

In big cities you find the usual department stores to do your shopping.

In all towns you also have supermarkets or discount shops. Most big shops in the city centres have opening hours from 9 to 18.30. Smaller shops open from 8–14 and 15–18.

On Saturdays all shops close at 14, but some may open as early as 8. The first Saturday of a month is a long shopping day from 8.30 – 16, 17 or 18.

Before you buy anything compare the prices. There may be differences in prices of up to 20 % for the same article.

And please, do not buy silly things like souvenirs: Lederhosen (leather shorts) or beer mugs with pictures on them etc. There is a lot of junk in souvenir shops.

3

Project 3

Focus on other countries

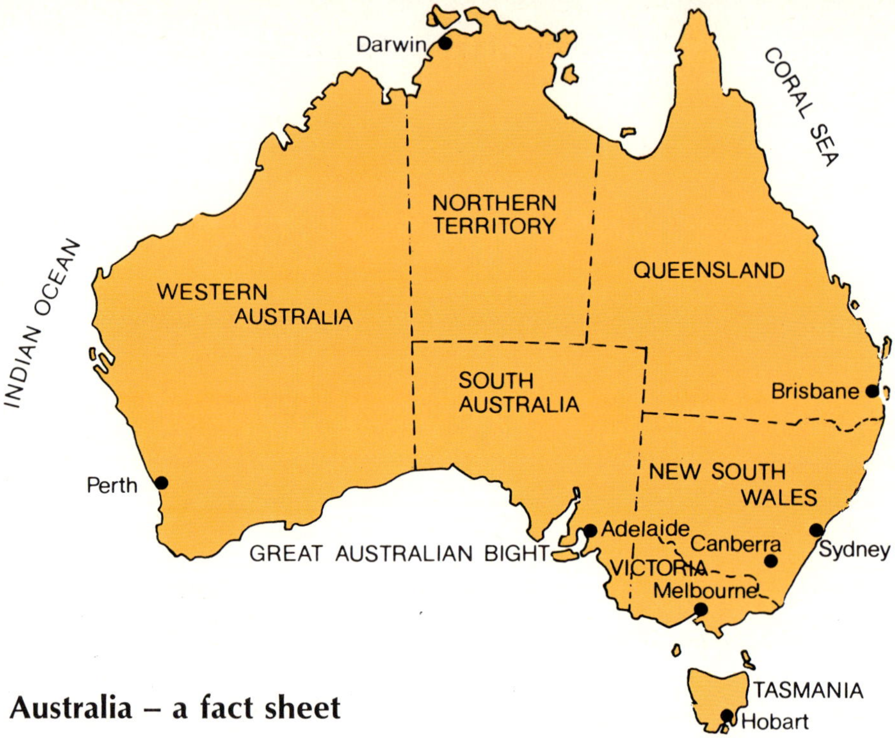

Australia – a fact sheet

Official Name:	Commonwealth of Australia	Capital City:	Canberra
		Official Language:	English
Government:	federal parliamentary	Official Religion:	none
		Area:	7,686,849 sq.km
Population:	approximately 14,400,000 British 95.6%, Italian 1.3%, Greek 0.9%, Dutch 0.4%, other 1.8% (including 139,000 Aboriginals)		

The first Australians – the Aboriginals

Before the Europeans settled in Australia, there were about 300,000 Aboriginals in over 500 different tribes speaking more than 200 different languages. The tribes were divided into families of 10 to 20, which lived by hunting and gathering fruit und roots. Their tools were very simple and usually made of wood, stone and bone. They had no kings. Decisions were made by the oldest and wisest men of the tribe. Animals, trees and holy places were very important in their religion.

The land of living fossils – Australia's strange fauna

Many of Australia's animals are very old species which can be found nowhere else in the world. For example:

The spiny anteater.

A small animal with spines rather like a hedgehog's. Eats mainly insects.

The platypus.

A furry animal with a bill like a duck's. The male has a poisonous spike on one of its back legs.

The kangaroo.

There are about 45 species of kangaroo. The largest, the red kangaroo, can be taller than a man. Eats grass. Sometimes a pest for farmers.

The koala.

Small animal like a bear. Does not drink water. Only eats the leaves of certain eucalyptus trees.

3

Project 3

Language study package

MINI MODEL TEXTS

I have read a lot about **Indians** and I have seen them in TV films. The word Indian reminds me of torture poles, buffalo hunting, beautiful sqaws, the prairie, wigwams, war dances and peace pipes. I do not think Indians have anything to do with New York, uranium pits and Canada.

The **first Americans** were Indians. They came to the American continent from Siberia. They moved through Alaska and spread throughout North and South America. They went in tribes. Each tribe had its own name, its own way of life, its own belief and its own language. When Columbus landed on the Bahamas he called the people there Indians because he thought he had landed in India. That is how the first Americans got the name Indians.

The Whites tried to make the Indians give up **their way of life.** They wanted them to live like the white people, to go farming, to work hard and to save money. But most of the Indians liked their own way of life. They did not want to live like the Whites.

WORDS

The	Indians	lived in		villages
Some	Whites	looked for		reservations
		went	for	tents
		used	to	wagons
		killed		new homes
		took away		west
		left	no	horses
			their	buffaloes
		. . .		land
				Indians
				soldiers
				guns

Using the Progressive

Read these mini-dialogues and

1. identify each verb: is it simple present or present progressive?
2. explain why simple present or present progressive is used.

. . .: What in the world are you doing?
. . .: Don't you have eyes? I'm washing my hair.
. . .: I can see that. Why are you using an egg?
. . .: I wash my hair with an egg every Friday night.
Eggs are good for your hair.

. . .: Where's Chuck? The movie starts at 7:30.
. . .: He always makes us late. Why can't he get ready on time just once?

You can also use the progressive for other tenses besides the present tense and the past tense.

Das Progressive zeigt für gewöhnlich die Dauer eines Ereignisses an und weist darauf hin, daß das Ereignis zeitlich begrenzt oder noch nicht beendet ist.

tense	progressive	
present	Peter **is writing** a letter	at the moment.
present perfect	Betty **has been writing** a letter	ever since she got home.
past	Tom **was writing** a letter	when the phone rang.
past perfect	Jane **had been writing** a letter	before the guests arrived.
future	Ben **will be writing** a letter	if we arrive at his house too early.
future perfect	Kate **will have been writing** a letter	while we were downtown.

Explain the use of the progressive in each of the example sentences: are the events described temporary or not yet completed?

progressive	tense form of BE	+ -ing form
present	am is are	
present perfect	have / has been	writing
past	was were	writing
past perfect	had been	writing
future	will be	writing
future perfect	will have been	

Possessive adjectives and possessive pronouns

. . .: I got my drinking straws at the supermarket.
Where did you get yours?
. . .: I got mine at the Hobby Centre.

▶
. . .: Our cassette recorder is broken. Can I borrow yours for my party?
. . .: Mine is broken, too. Ask Chuck if you can borrow his.

▶
. . .: Have you seen Carol's robot mask?
. . .: I haven't seen hers, but Janie and Martha showed me theirs yesterday.

A reminder

personal pronouns	possessive adjectives	possessive pronouns
I	my	mine
you	your	yours
he	his	his
she	her	hers
it	its	its
we	our	ours
you	your	yours
they	their	theirs

Possession practice

Put the correct possessive adjective or possessive pronoun into each blank.

John made . . . robot mask at home.

Where did you finish . . .?
I finished . . . in our garden last night.

I made . . . experiment at home yesterday.
. . . worked out well.
But Tom said . . . didn't work out well.

Carola thinks . . . was very exciting.

. . . Father was most surprised.

Using language to compare: practice

Use this language material to form at least 16 sentences.
Use the language of comparison.

the Mississippi River	big	Lake Constance
Lake Superior	small	Frankfurt
Mt. McKinley	long	Germans
New York	tall	the Washington Monument
Disney World	exciting	the Rhine River
Americans	tasty	the Zugspitze
hamburgers	crowded	pizza
My sentences	good	yours
My jeans	right	hers

Comparison of adverbs

Ken played carelessly.
Ron played more carelessly.
Steve played most carelessly.

The Rams played brilliantly.
The Lions played more brilliantly.
The Steelers played most brilliantly.

Comparison of adverbs		
positive	comparative	superlative
quickly	more quickly	most quickly
carelessly	more carelessly	most carelessly
The comparison of adverbs ending in **-ly** is formed with **more, most.**		

Note: early, earlier, earliest

Anything you can do, I can do better

In groups of three, practise bragging about what you can do.

Example: I sing beautifully.
I sing more beautifully.
I sing most beautifully.

Here are a few things to brag about. Try to think of more.

run quickly
dance brilliantly
tell stories excitingly
dress nicely
talk interestingly
spend money carefully

4 Inventions and Ideas

Project 4

Starters

How does each invention work?

Are these inventions practical?

Would you like to have any of them?

Give each invention a name.

1. Write down what you believe to be the five most important inventions ever made.
2. Compare you list with those of your classmates. With your class make a count of the inventions and how many times each appears on a list. Draw up a frequency table.

Important inventions

Johannes Gutenberg

Rudolf Diesel

Wilbur and Orville Wright

Joseph and Jacques Montgolfier

James Watt

(invention) WHAT?	(person responsible) BY WHOM?	(country) WHERE?	(year) WHEN?
diesel engine		Germany	1892
dynamite		Sweden	1867
telephone	Alexander Graham Bell	Britain	1876
engine (petrol)		Germany	1883
television	John Logie Baird	Britain	1926
radium		France	1898
gramophone	Thomas Alva Edison	U.S.A.	1877
lightning conductor		U.S.A.	1752
penicillin		Britain	1928
pendulum clock	Christian Huygens	Netherlands	1673
postage stamp	Sir Rowland Hill	Britain	1840
printing		Germany	1436
wireless telegraphy	Guglielmo Marconi	Italy	1896
steam turbine	Sir Charles A. Parsons	Britain	1884
X-rays		Germany	1895
atomic structure	Lord Rutherford	Britain	1911
balloon		France	1783
photography	J. Niecéphore Niepce	France	1822
typewriter	Christopher Sholes	U.S.A.	1862
steam locomotive	Richard Trevithick	Britain	1803
steam engine		Britain	1765
aeroplane		U.S.A.	1903

Alfred Nobel

Wilhelm Roentgen

Benjamin Franklin

Carl Benz and Gottlieb Daimler

Sir Alexander Fleming

Pierre and Marie Curie

Get organized

The world's most and least important inventions

Please, rank the 12 most and
the 12 in your opinion least important
inventions.

What do you think? Rank the inventions in order of importance (from the most to the least important).

most important for us — least important in my opinion

Compare and discuss your scales.

Are there important inventions which are not in the list?
Maybe from very early times? (the wheel, the bucket, the knife, . . .)

FIRST AID

W R O N G !

Language aids

I think . . . is	important.
	not important.
	very important.

Without it	men	couldn't live.	
		would die of	hunger.
			cold.
			illness.

. . .	people couldn't	travel	as much	as they do now.
		eat . . .	as far	
		buy . . .		
		. . .		

. . .	people would have to work much	longer	to get . . .
		harder	
		more	

. . .	we wouldn't	hear	what	is going on	far away.
		see		has gone on	in . . .
		know			

. . . people couldn't . . . at all.

Can you think of inventions for the future? Of things which have not yet been invented but might be useful for survival?

4

Project 4

Inventions

❶ The boy who invented the Bubble Gun

1st "DAD, CAN I SPEAK TO YOU?"
"WELL, WHAT DO YOU WANT?"
Julian held out his diagram. "LOOK DAD,
I HAVE INVENTED A BUBBLE GUN."
"HA HA, WHAT GOOD IS THAT?"
"I WILL MAKE A LOT OF MONEY WITH IT."
"OH, FOR GODSSAKE, CAN'T YOU SEE I'M BUSY?"
"BUT LOOK, DAD, I'M GOING TO MAKE A MILLION DOLLARS".
"WELL THEN, COME BACK WHEN YOU'VE GOT THE MILLION DOLLARS AND STOP BOTHERING ME NOW."

2nd Dear Mom, don't worry about me.
I've gone to sell my Bubble Gun invention.
I will make a lot of money.
Dad only laughed at me about it.
I've taken the money
Grandma gave me for my birthday
and some underwear.
Love Julian
P.S. Don't worry. I took some stuff
for sandwiches.

3rd His mother now pointed an accusing
finger at his father.
"YOU'VE DRIVEN OUR CHILD FROM HIS HOME."
"OH, NO I DIDN'T."
"OH, YES YOU DID."
"OH, NO I DIDN'T."
"OH, YES YOU DID."
"WHAT WILL HAPPEN TO HIM!
HE WILL STARVE."
His father pointed at the note.
"HE SAID HE TOOK SOME STUFF FOR SANDWICHES."
"JULIAN, JULIAN.
OH MY GOD, HE'S JUST A BABY."

4th There were two drawings.
THE BUBBLE GUN

1. Soapy solution compartment
2. Trigger-actuated soapy solution pump
3. Soapy solution hose
4. Bubble-making ring
5. Soapy solution fill-up plug
6. Rubber air bag
7. Trigger-actuated air bag compressor
8. Air nozzle

OPERATION

Compressing the trigger,
the soapy solution will be drawn
to the bubble ring.
The air bag will be compressed,
releasing the air through the nozzle.
This air will produce a bubble
when going through the bubble making ring.

In the lower-right-hand corner was printed,
THE BUBBLE GUN, INVENTED BY JULIAN WEST,
137 EAST VIEW TERRACE, SAN DIEGO,
CALIFORNIA, APRIL 25, 1973.

Paul Gallico

Questions

– Can you draw the bubble gun?
– Is it possible to make a million dollars by producing and selling bubble guns?
– Would you buy a bubble gun?
– Would you give away a bubble gun as a present?

– What do you think about the father's reaction?
– Have you ever thought of running away from home?
– If so why?
– Do you think a little boy could survive having run away from home?

– Is it a story in British or in American English?
– Do you know any other stories of Paul Gallico?
– Are there any of his books in your public library?

Note-making III – the headline-method

Look at the story again.
Choose a headline for each of the five paragraphs;
it might be a sentence from the paragraph, for example:

1. "I have invented a bubble gun"
2. . . .

. . .

Now shut the book and tell the story in simple sentences using your headlines. You might begin like this:

The boy told his father: "I have invented a bubble gun."
But the father wouldn't listen.
. . .

② A man of science

1847–1931

As a child in Ohio, U.S.A., Thomas Alva Edison made an experiment with two cats.

He tied two of their legs together with wire and tried to generate electricity by stroking them.

To improve Bell's telephone he invented the carbon microphone. The carbon disc transmits the sound of the voice as electricity.

He produced the first phonograph. The machine was no good for him because from early childhood he could not hear very well.

Later he invented the first talking doll by using the phonograph.

He needed many experiments to solve another problem: making an electric light shine for a long time.* At last he used carbonized bamboo. That did the trick: He had made the first commercial electric light.

* A German, Alfred Goebel, from Springe, Germany, had invented an electric bulb, but it did not glow for a long time.

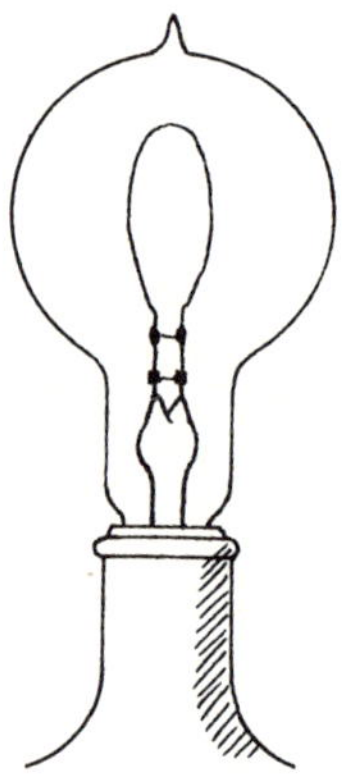

Task

Make up sentences using

. . . was invented by . . .
. . . were tied up with . . .
. . . was generated by . . .
. . .'s . . . was improved by . . .

The . . . of . . . were transmitted by. . .
as . . .

The . . . was used for . . .
A . . . of . . . were needed by . . . to . . .
The first . . . had been invented . . .,
but the first commercial . . .

Discuss:

What is the difference between the sentences in the texts and in the tasks? Note every detail.

3 You can be an inventor

Inventing needs much practising.

Here is your chance.

Divide the square into four equal parts.

Think of as many uses as you can for this brick.

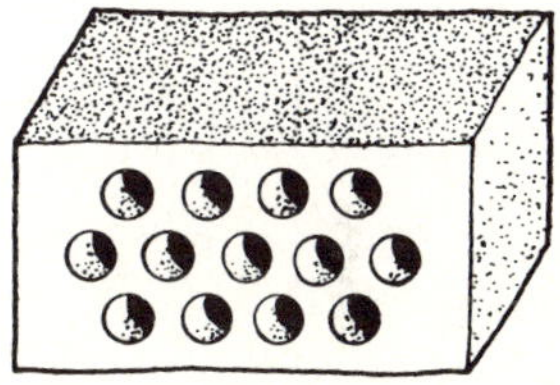

Write at least 20 words using only the letters from this word.
Each new word must have at least three letters.

GENERATOR

Moving only three matches, make the point of the pyramid point down.

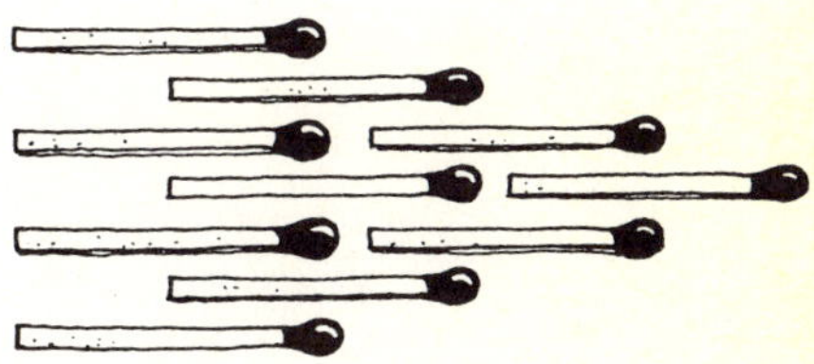

You can make the front of the house face west if you move only one match.

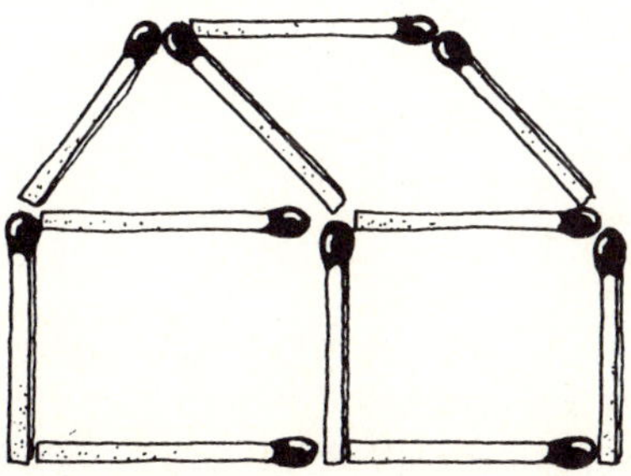

Everyday inventions

Inventions are madé not only by scientists, engineers or geniuses, but also by people like you and me.
Every day you invent something –
perhaps the solution to one of these problems:

How do you make a table stand even?

How do you carry a hot pot without burning yourself?

How do you get into your flat when you don't have a key?

Tasks 1. Complete a table like the one below. Describe how you would solve each of these problems.

Problem	Tools, Equipment	Number of people	Procedure	Special Considerations
Making table stand even	thick piece of paper (folded) book ...	1 2 if it is heavy	First: find out which leg is too short second: ...	Be sure other legs don't become too short ...

2. Find out how your classmates would solve these problems. Are any of their ideas better than yours? Which ones? Why?

Your comments in good English

Language aids

agree

I think	you're	right.
	he's	
	she's	

I agree with ...
That's right.
... may be right.

disagree

Are you sure?
I'm afraid you're wrong.
I'm afraid you're mistaken.
I think you are quite wrong.
I can't agree with you there.
Impossible.

3. Give a talk about the best method to make a table stand even, or about one of the other problems.
Use the headings in the table above and your notes.

4 What is it all about?

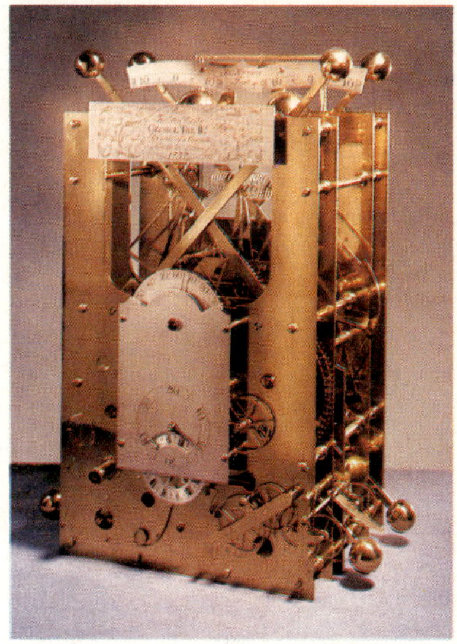

Harrison's first chronometer

water
radio
watch
Jerry Lewis
England
fast
old
Cape Canaveral
spacecraft
museum
clock
longitude
bombs
1850
hobby
model
east
maps
navigation
position

Harrison's fourth chronometer

physics
bigger planes
workshop
school
astrology
small
inventions
medicine
clockmaker
geography
time
presents
thermometer
NATO
expensive
chronometer
electricity
1650
Jamaica
west
Rolls Royce
astronomy

It has | something / nothing | to do with . . .

. . . has . . . to do with . . .
I'm sure the objects have . . .

I think it has | nothing / something | . . . .

Get the facts about the chronometer.

The Marine Chronometer

Ever since the beginning of sea travel,
navigators had had problems   people at the steering wheel
when they tried to determine   know
a ship's position east or west.
They needed a clock
that would keep good time.
Even an error of two minutes   mistake
would put a ship 30 miles off course.   away from
In 1714, after a flagship had been wrecked on the Scilly Islands,
(the captain thought he was sailing up the English Channel),
the British Admiralty set up a Board of Longitude to   committee
offer a prize of £ 20,000 for a clock
with an error of less than two minutes
on a trip to the West Indies and back.

John Harrison (1693–1776),
a Yorkshire carpenter,
entered his first clock or chronometer   sent in
for the prize in 1735.
He spent the next 30 years improving it.   making it better
He reduced its size from the 72 pounds   made it smaller
of his first model to the model in 1761,
which had the size of a clock.
His son took this model on a test trip
under the supervision of an astronomer.   watched by
After a voyage lasting 81 days,
the ship reached Jamaica,
where the chronometer was found
to be only five seconds slow.
Captain Cook took a copy of this model
on his second voyage around the world in 1772–75.
It was only 7 minutes 45 seconds slow
after three years at sea in temperatures
ranging from tropical to polar.
But the Admiralty refused to   would not
pay the full prize money.
The 80 year old inventor appealed to the king.   called for help
George III said, "By God, Harrison, I'll see you righted".
Even then Harrison did not get the full prize.

John Harrison had worked all his life for his chronometer. On March 24, 1776, he died at the age of eighty-three in Red Lion Square, London.

Adapted from EUREKA ed. Edward de Bono 1974 Thames and Hudson, Ltd. London.

Classroom discourse

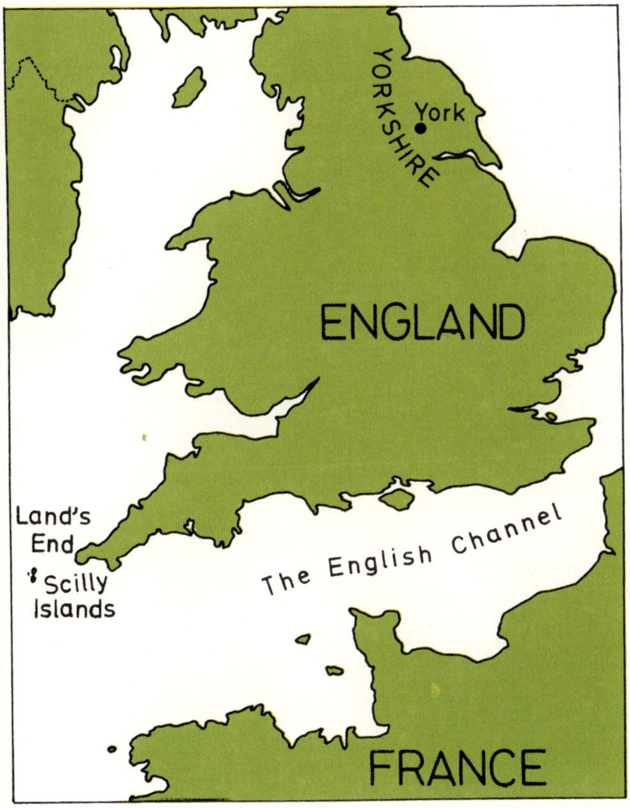

Can I ask a question?

Excuse me, what does . . . . mean?

Sorry, I didn't understand.

Could Can	you	repeat that, please say that again speak up a little	? .

Sorry, can you explain that again?

Please	repeat the last	sentence. word.
	write this word on the board.	

Did you say . . .?

I'd we'd	like to rather	do read work on start on work with . . .	. . .

What are we	going to supposed to	do? read? . . .
How are we	going to supposed to	report?

Some facts from another point of view

Who was it?

Harrison? Harrison's son? The king?
The astronomer? The Board of Longitude?

You are the detective.

1

Clock-maker and carpenter

Who was it?

2

Who were they?

They always found reasons to keep the prize money.

3

Who was he?

He could not leave his chronometer alone. It had become part of his existence. He started to take it apart to see if he could improve the mechanism. He made various small changes which he thought would increase the accurary of the chronometer. Finally he got it working well.

4

Who did it?

He found that the chronometer was almost 100 per cent accurate and ordered that the Board give the money to Harrison at once.

5

Who went?

He went on another voyage to the West Indies on March 28, 1764. The four months' voyage across the Atlantic Ocean was often rough and stormy. In that kind of weather only the very best chronometer was reliable.

6

Who was it?

He took a copy of Harrison's model on a voyage around the world.

7

Who were they?

But they still kept the prize money.

8

Who said this to whom?

"I want you to take the chronometer on another sea voyage. I think you will probably find an improvement in its performance."

9

Who?

He was so angry that he went directly to the King, who said that Harrison should put one of the chronometers in the Royal Observatory at Richmond, where the King would test it himself.

Language aids

I believe . . .
I think . . .
I suppose . . .

Maybe it was . . .
It might have been . . .

Find the answers on page 74.

5 Think and talk about the reading passage

Note-making IV: the WHO did WHAT method

Look at each paragraph of the reading passage about the marine chronometer and make notes using a table like this one:

WHO?	did WHAT?	WHEN?	WHERE?

Then shut your book and use your notes to make a time line, beginning with the year of Harrison's birth and ending with his death.

Points for discussion

1. What was the conflict between Harrison and the Board of Longitude?
2. Why did Harrison think he should get the prize money?
   Write a letter to the Board demanding the money.
   Use the information from the reading passage about the success of the chronometer as evidence.
3. When should the Board have given Harrison the money?
   What do you think?
4. Based on the information in the reading passages, choose words from this list that describe Harrison.

   careless crazy (mad) successful clever intelligent
   patient dishonest rich arrogant creative trustworthy

Talking about the time

... Can you tell me the time please?
... Sorry. I don't have a watch on.

... My watch has stopped.
Can you tell me the exact time?
... Certainly. It's exactly 23 minutes after three.

... According to the clock on the bank, it's only six fifteen.
... It always runs slow. Don't rely on it.

... Hello. May I help you?
... Yes, please. My watch has stopped and I can't make it start.
... That's because you have overwound it.

... It says in the Frankfurt newspaper that the concert starts at 20:00. That's funny.
... What's so funny about that?
... In the United States nobody says "20:00". We say eight o'clock.
... What if it's not clear if you mean morning or afternoon?
... Then we say a.m. for morning and p.m. for evening.

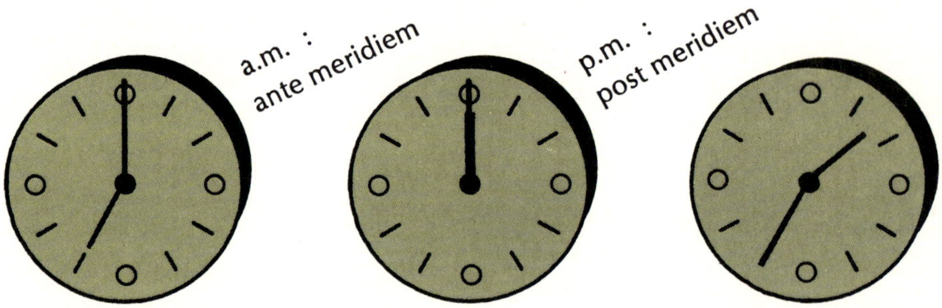

Thinking about time

1. Where might each of the conversations above have taken place? Who is speaking?
2. What other words and expressions do you know to talk about the time?
3. How many different ways are there to say the time as shown on each clock?

   How do English speakers distinguish between 5 o'clock in the morning and 5 o'clock in the afternoon?

   What do p.m. and a.m. stand for?
4. Which time zone do you live in?

   How many time zones would you cross if you flew from Frankfurt to Hong Kong? To New York? To Capetown?

Everybody an inventor

NECESSITY IS THE MOTHER OF INVENTION.

1. You are a babysitter and can't leave the house. You see smoke coming from a window opposite, and there is no telephone.
2. You want to go and see someone who lives on the first floor of a house. There is no bell at the garden gate, and there is a horribly big dog between the gate and the main entrance.

Can you invent something to make yourself seen or heard?
Can you explain the meaning of the proverb above?

4

At the post office

Keep in touch with home –
post and telephone
help you to communicate –
hear the latest, make a date!

Project 4

Focus on Germany

Where and how you can make a telephone call

You can make a telephone call from any post office or from any of the many yellow call boxes. You can phone from your hotel too, of course; however, it is advisable to make enquiries there beforehand about the extra charges to be paid in addition to the official charges.

You will recognize the call boxes from which you can make calls also to other countries by the green sign.

You will find one of the two kinds of payphone depicted below:

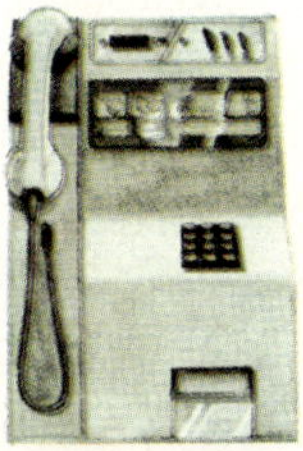

-,10 1,- 5,-

a.) for calls to all countries with STD

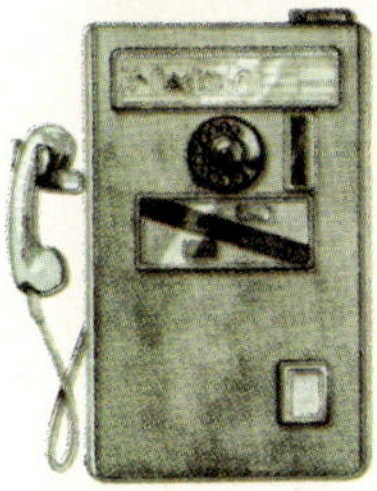

-,10 -,50 1,-

b.) for subscriber-dialled calls to all European countries.

Do you need stamps?
Would you like to send a telegram?
Do you want to make a phone call?
No problem.
Just go to the post office.
You can't miss it. Look for
the colour yellow.

Often the post people speak English.
But you will also find information
sheets, leaflets or brochures
in English.

Unfortunately the counters have
German words only.
WERTZEICHEN means stamps.
FERNSPRECHER means telephone.
FERNSPRECHBUCH means telephone directory.
WERTZEICHENGEBER is stamp machine.
FERNMÜNDLICH means by telephone.

4

Project 4

Focus on other countries

Matching words

In CONTACTS 8 BC and in this book you had to read and to listen to texts in British and in American English. (BE and AE)
Here is a list of BE and AE words. Find a German correspondent for each pair of words.

BRITISH	AMERICAN	GERMAN
aerial (radio/TV)	antenna	...
anorak	parka	...
autumn	fall	...
bank note	bill	
billion = million million	billion = thousand million	
biscuit (sweet)	cookie	
biscuit (unsweetened)	cracker	
bonnet (car)	hood	
boot (car)	trunk	
caravan	trailer	
centre (city)	downtown	
chairmann (business)	President	
chemist's shop	pharmacy/drugstore	
chips	French fries	
chocolate/sweets	candy	
crisps (potato)	chips	
cupboard	closet	
curtains	drapes	
dustbin	garbage/trash can	
first floor	second floor	
flat	apartment	
a fortnight	two weeks	
full stop	period	
garden	yard	
handbag	purse	
holiday	vacation	
lavatory/loo/w.c.	toilet/john/bathroom	
lift	elevator	
motorway	freeway	
pack (cards)	deck	
parcel	package	
pavement	sidewalk	
petrol	gas	
tube	subway	
wash up	do the dishes	
wash your hands	wash up	

Halloween

Halloween is a fine day for children. They go in costumes from door to door. They shout, "Trick or treat." Or: "Shell-out, shell-out." They want people to give them treats. You can give them nuts or sweets. You should wrap them in paper first. Some children collect money for UNICEF (United Nations Children's Fund).

Adults also celebrate Halloween. They hold parties and dress up in costumes. Halloween has a long history which goes back to the Romans. At this time of the

year they honoured the goddess of the fruit trees. Years later, in England, people held a religious feast at this time of year in honour of the Christian saints. This feast was called the Feast of All Saints. The word "Halloween" meant "holy evening" – the evening before the Feast of All Saints.

Today Halloween is not a religious holiday any more. It is a time for fun. A long time ago people believed that on Halloween the spirits of dead people came back to visit their homes. Nowadays people dress

up as ghosts. You can also see black cats and witches on broomsticks. Many people make a Jack o'Lantern: they clean out the inside of a pumpkin. Then they cut out a face and put a candle inside. What a ghost!

Task When do children go from house to house in Germany to ask for treats?

Language aids

They | want / ask | people to give . . .

If people don't . . . .

they | will / may | . . .

4

Project 4

Language study package

MINI MODEL TEXTS

The **inventions** shown as starters are very funny. I like the swimcycle and the umbrelhat best of all. The walkcycle is not bad, either. The pedallift is a great invention. So is the wheelpiano. A sitskirt is nice, too. I wish I could invent something.

Some inventions are **not very interesting.** For example I could live without dynamite and the steam locomotive, I think. I could do without nuclear power. The least important invention is make-up.

WORDS

Engines			for seeing in the dark
Telephones			for knowing what's going on far away
Record players			for getting from one place to another one
Tape recorders			for getting food
Grammophones	is	important	for packing food
Radios	are	useful	for making hard work easy
Television	isn't	necessary	for being in time
Clocks	aren't	used	for getting to places in time
Photography			for getting food from the supermarket
Airplanes			to keep alive
Lights			for eating
Motor cars			for keeping records
Bombs			for entertainment
Ships			for boring evenings
Clothes			for saving time
Knives			for saving money
Baskets			
Bags			
Boxes			

Possessive pronouns

Jack and I made . . . robot together,
. . . was the best of all.
Paul, Jane, Henry and I built . . . dream castle in ten minutes.
. . . came out third, but . . . story got the first prize.

▶

Where did you park . . . bikes this morning?
Hans parked . . . in front of the school, but we left . . . on the bus parking lot.
Be careful. I left . . . there yesterday and somebody stole it.

▶

I'm going to get . . . hair cut at Jacobson's this afternoon.
Elfi got . . . cut there last week. It looks great.
Where do you usually get . . . cut?
. . . sister always cuts it.

▶

Using Interrogative Pronouns

Make up eight interview questions for a classmate:

Try to find out something new about him or her.
If you like, prepare a short report about him or her.
Use each of the following interrogatives at least once:

For example:

what (what colour or what food)	which
when	who
where	how

What did you talk **about?**
Where are you **from?**
Who did you go to the game **with?**

Wenn in einer WH-Frage (Frage mit when, where, who, what, which, how) zu dem Fragewort ein Verhältniswort gehört, so steht das Verhältniswort normalerweise am Ende des Satzes.

Fill in the missing words in these mini-dialogues between teachers and students.

. . .: I can't remember where we were when class ended yesterday.
. . . were we talking . . .?
. . .: We were talking about John Harrison.

. . .: I can't find my math notebook. Have you seen it?
. . .: . . . does it look . . .?
. . .: It's red and blue and has an American flag on the back.

. . .: Birgit, where's your workbook?
. . .: I don't have it. I lent it to Harry and he put it away.
. . .: Well, Harry, . . . did you put it?

. . .: Excuse me. Are you Mr Berger? I'm Uwe Schmitt, the new student.
. . .: Hello, Uwe. We're glad to have you. . . . are you . . .?
. . .: From Berlin.

. . .: Mr Berger, . . . page was our homework . . .?
. . .: On page 290, Renate. Does that mean that you didn't do your homework last night?

. . .: Walter, I want you and one other student to prepare a short talk on European team handball.
. . . would you like to work . . .?
. . .: With Georg, Mr Berger.

Question tags

It was dangerous to go down Niagara Falls, wasn't it?
They must have been crazy, mustn't they?
You wouldn't do that, would you?

It doesn't pay to do silly things, does it?
A lot of people like risks, don't they?
They never miss a chance to do silly things, do they?

A conversation

Visitor:	It's very hot the whole year round, . . .?
Australian:	Yes, it is. But you like it, . . .?
Visitor:	Oh yes, fantastic. Surfing's your great hobby, . . .?
Australian:	Yes, it is. You have never tried it, . . .?
Visitor:	No, I haven't. It is not easy, . . .?
Australian:	Well, I don't know. I don't think it is very difficult. You'd like to try, . . .?
Visitor:	Yes, I would. Ah, that's a platypus, . . .?
Australian:	Yes, you are right. There aren't any platypusses in Germany, . . .?
Visitor:	No, there aren't. They don't bite, . . .?
Australian:	I don't think so.
Visitor:	That restaurant is open, . . .?
Australian:	Yes, it is. We could have a quick lunch, . . .?
Visitor:	Good Idea.
Australian:	You like wine, . . .?
Visitor:	Yes, but it's very expensive over here, . . .?
Australian:	No, it isn't.
Visitor:	But you must import it, . . .?
Australian:	Oh no, we needn't, we produce our own wine.
Visitor:	Indeed? I'd like to taste it.
Australian:	Red or white?
Visitor:	White, please. It's dry, . . .?
Australian:	Yes, most of our wines are dry. German wines aren't dry, . . .?
Visitor:	We have dry wines, too. But a lot of people prefer sweet wine.

Note

Positive statement	——→	negative tag	Negative statement	——→	positive tag
You like sweets,		don't you?	You don't like sweets,		do you?

Using singular and plural forms

List the singular and plural forms which belong together.

geese matches fish boss bushes roofs fish match life
cheeseburger secretary donkeys sheep mouse secretaries sheep
chiefs children monkeys lives deer knives feet mice
foot roof puppies bosses cheeseburgers

Ask you know the plural forms of some nouns are not simply the noun + **s.**

1. Find the plural forms above which do not have a matching singular. What is the singular for each?
2. Put the nouns into groups according to their plural forms. Find other nouns for each group.

Rewrite the following sentences.

Change the singular nouns to plural and the plural nouns to singular.

Put the **loaf** of bread on the **shelf** in the kitchen.
The **children** often eat **cheeseburgers** at hamburger **restaurants.**
If your **tooth** hurts, don't eat those candy **bars.**
Would you like a **tomato** with your **sandwich**?
Everyone knows that **mice** like to eat cheese.
Please hand me the **knife**. I want to cut these **bananas**.
Be careful! A **potato** is falling out of your basket.
When an American **mother** goes to the grocery **store,**
she often buys a **box** of cornflakes and a **jar** of peanut butter.
Would you **puppy** like to eat this lettuce **leaf**?
Have you **brothers** caught any **fish** yet?

Words only used in the plural

a) articles consisting of two equal parts

pyjamas	Schlafanzug	glasses	Brille	pliers	(Kneif-) Zange
shorts	kurze Hose	scales	Waage	scissors	Schere
jeans	Jeans				
trousers	lange Hose			tongs	Zange

c) some words not ending in **-s**

arms	Waffen	customs	Zoll	regards	Grüße
clothes	Kleidung	goods	Waren	riches	Reichtum
contents	Inhalt	minutes	Protokoll	stairs	Treppe

b) some words ending is **-s**

cattle	Vieh	police	Polizei
people	Leute		

5 Violence

Project 5

Starters

An aggressiveness test

1. If you find someone stealing apples from your trees, would you
   a) phone the police?
   b) make him give back your apples?
   c) tell him to go away, but let him keep a few?
2. Your girlfriend or boyfriend is late for a date. You would say:
   a) "You're late!"
   b) "Where have you been all this time?"
   c) "I was beginning to get worried about you!"
3. When you are playing a game,
   a) is it important for you to win?
   b) do you play 'just for the fun of it'?
   c) do you hate losing?
4. In a crowd someone steps on your foot and says, 'I'm sorry'. You would say:
   a) "It's O.K. It was my fault anyway."
   b) "That's O.K. Forget it."
   c) "Why don't you look where you're going?"
5. If you had to be reborn as an animal, would you rather be
   a) a leopard?
   b) a house cat?
   c) an elephant?

You've probably seen quizzes like this before.

They usually have several multiple choice questions and then a key in which the answers are analysed.

In small groups make up a key for this quiz. Give the most aggressive answer for each question 3 points, the next most aggressive answer 2 points and the least aggressive answer 1 point.

1	a ( )	b ( )	c ( )
2	a ( )	b ( )	c ( )
3	a ( )	b ( )	c ( )
4	a ( )	b ( )	c ( )
5	a ( )	b ( )	c ( )

'CRAZY' HELL'S ANGEL IS JAILED 15 YEARS

A HELL'S ANGELS' leader was jailed for 15 years yesterday.

By JOHN HILL

Bearded "Crazy Ken" Littlefield was found guilty of attempted murder.

And prison sentences totalling 64 years were slapped on 23 other Angels.

Mr Justice Sheldon told them at the end:

"If you believe yourselves to be above the law and able to do as you please, you are wrong."

The 24 leather clad thugs are part of the "All-England" Hell's Angels' chapter.

Their rivals, the Windsor chapter, had refused to join a federation of motorbike gangs.

The All-England mob attacked them with shotguns, knives and iron bars.

One of the raiders shot the Windsors' leader Richard Sharman in the head.

Littlefield was said to have ordered the shooting.

Sharman survived but police never found the man who pulled the trigger.

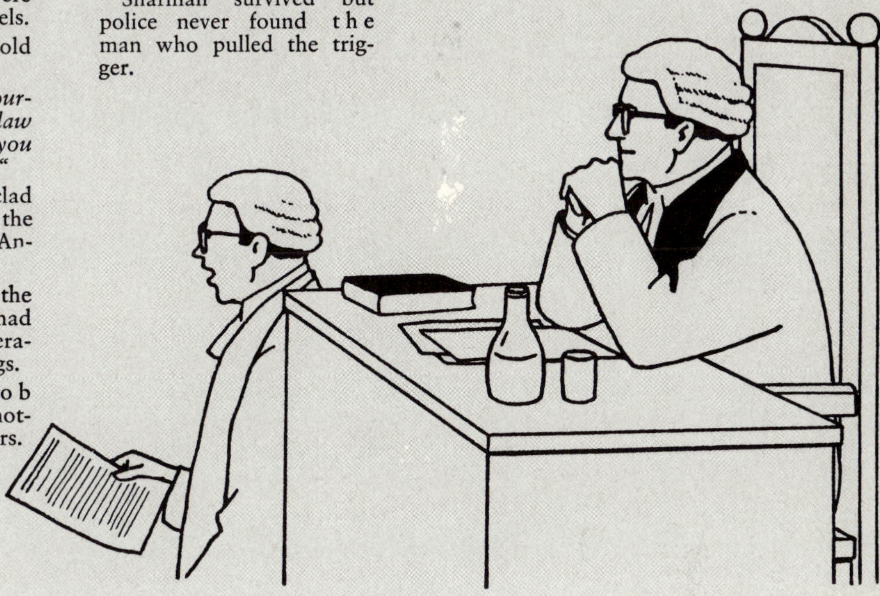

Tip This is an authentic newspaper article.
You may not understand it at once.
Here is a little trick: Write all the words that **you do understand** on a sheet of paper.
Try and understand the facts from your notes.

Think and talk about the reading passage

- What were the names of the two gangs?
- What were the names of their leaders?
- Who was the aggressor (that means: which gang attacked the other one)?
- Why?
- Who was shot?
- How many years of prison did Crazy Ken get?
- The judge told the gang members that they have to obey the law. What were his exact words?

5

Project 5

Violence

❶ How aggressive can you get?

most aggressive

fairly aggressive

not aggressive

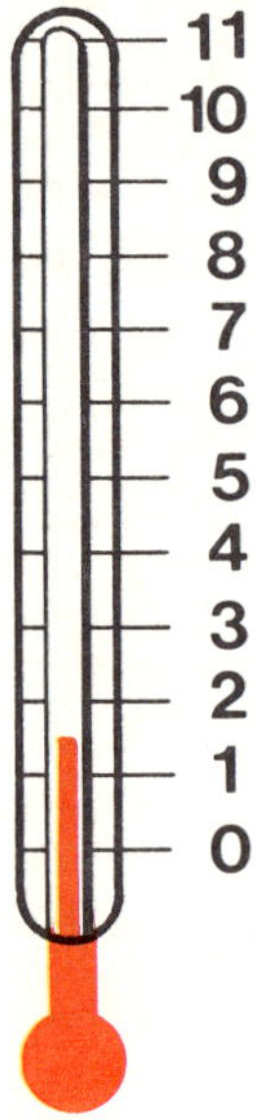

Where would you put these words on the aggressometer
Put them into rank order from the least aggressive to the most aggressive.
Use a dictionary to find out.

- furious
- calm
- angry
- cool
- irate
- wild
- nervous
- ill-tempered
- mad
- self-controlled

People are aggressive when they

- talk to their brother
- ride a (motor) bike
- talk to their sister
- feel lonely
- dance in a disco
- have a flat tyre
- watch football
- hear rock music
- watch a play
- have to speak English
- cannot find something
- have no cigarettes
- are hungry
- see a dog
- watch TV
- play football
- do not get what they want
- see a policeman
- didn't sleep well
- see the school building
- have had a bad test
- see their . . . teacher
- are tired
- see a cat

Or: I never feel aggressive.
The most aggressive . . . I know is . . .

❷ The bank robber

Tell the story about father and son and the bank robber.

Language aids

- knock down
- point the gun at the bank clerks
- carry on their shoulders
- reporters

Tasks Write the story down.
Can you explain at what point the different people in the story got aggressive?
Whose aggressiveness did you like? Why?
Whose aggressiveness didn't you like? Why?

3

Sunset in Biafra

'Put down your bag,' he said. 'I want to search you.'

I obeyed. He rummaged° through my handbag.

'Strip!°'

'Surely you can search me without my stripping?'

'Strip!'

I removed my shirt.

'Off with your trousers!'

'What is all this?'

'Off with your trousers, I say!'

The detainees° looked at me sadly. There were three women among them. One of them had a child of about three with her. She sighed.

I removed my trousers.

'Now search me,' I said coldly.

'Off with your pants!'

I was surprised. I did not move. Anger began to well up° in me. I fought to control it.

'Do you suppose I can hide a gun inside my pants?'

'Off with your pants, I say!'

There was silence. My fellow detainees watched in frozen attention.

He cocked° his machine gun and pointed it at my legs. The fellow might shoot to save his pride; not to kill, perhaps, but to injure. It had happened many times already.

'Now strip, I say.'

I stripped.

(Elechi Amadi, Sunset in Biafra)

Language aids

rummaged: hunted
strip: undress, take ones clothes off
detainees: prisoners
well up: rise, go up
cocked: prepared (for shooting)

Think and talk about the reading passage

- Why should the man with the gun want to kill or injure a prisoner "to save his pride"?
- Did the other man feel aggressive, too?
- What made him angry?
- Why didn't he show his anger?
- Why did the others watch in "frozen attention"?
- Find a headline for the story. Try to show in this headline what the story is about.

How to control aggressiveness

I think, the best method to control aggressiveness is

- talking to a friend
- working it out by physical exercise (jogging, cycling)
- thinking of something else (reading, watching TV)
- writing it down in a letter or diary
- taking a hot bath
- taking a cold shower
- praying

...

Do you remember the article about Ken Littlefield and the judge?
Here are three dialogues from another court of justice.
If you don't understand them ask questions.

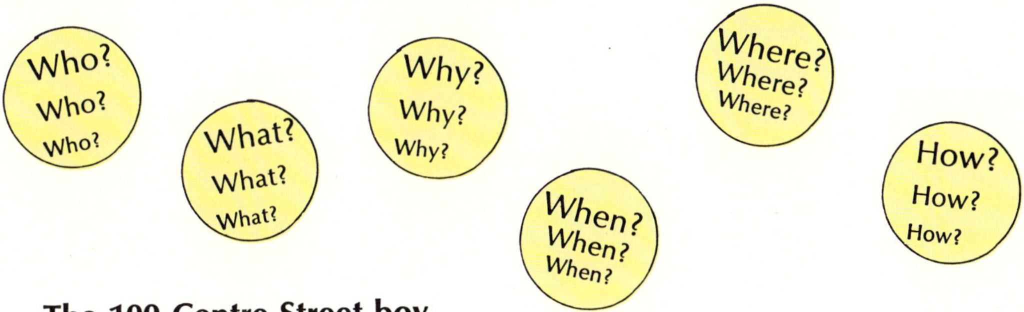

4 The 100 Centre Street boy

1. "You speak English?"
   "Yes, Sir."
   "Speak up. I can't hear you
   You speak English!?"
   "Yes, Sir."
   "You can't afford a lawyer."
   "No, Sir."
   "O.K, Legal aid.
   Put him in.
   Next case."

2. "Stand up straight
   and take your hands
   out of the pockets."
   "Yes, Sir."
   "Where's your family?
   Why isn't your family here?"
   "My mother works."
   "What's that? Speak up."
   "My mother works."
   "Well, doesn't she know
   that you're in serious trouble?
   We all work,
   but doesn't she know
   she has an obligation to this court
   to be here?"
   "Yes, Sir."
   "Well you can just wait.
   You go back and wait
   and we'll give your mother time to come.
   Call the case later."
   "But my mother's at work."
   "Call the next case."

3. "What's this? A sentence?"
   "Yes, your Honour."
   "Any motions?"
   "No, your Honour.
   I'd just like to say:
   The boy does have a job
   and this is his first offence."
   "Shoplifting is theft, Mr. Defence Attorney,
   are you aware of that?"
   "Yes, Sir."
   "Six months in the city prison.
   Call the next case."

Perhaps you could act those scenes.

You need the judge,
the defence attorney,
and three boys.

Before you start, discuss:

- What is the first boy's name?
- Where is he from?
- What language(s) does he speak?
- How many brothers and sisters has he got?
- What's his offence?
  How does he feel?
- And the second boy?
- And the third boy?
- What can you say about the defence attorney?
- And the judge?

5 Violence on TV

The following table lists the programs shown during prime time (8.00 p. m.–11:00 p. m.) in one week on the three national networks of American television.

	PROGRAM TITLE	KIND OF PROGRAM	PROGRAM TIME (in minutes)
Saturday	Jeffersons	comedy	30
	Emergency!	doctor series	60
	Good Heavens	comedy	30
	Eyewitness Magazine	news	30
	Pilot	comedy	30
	All American Football Game	sports	120
	Mary Tyler Moore	comedy	30
	Movie: "Charro"	western	120
	Bob Newhart	comedy	30
	Dinah Shore	musical variety	60
Sunday	Sonny and Cher	musical variety	60
	Six Million Dollar Man	adventure	60
	Ellery Queen	mystery	60
	Kojak	crime drama	60
	The Last Detail	comedy	60
	U.S. Olympic Trials	sports	90
	Columbo	crime drama	60
	Bronk	crime drama	60
Monday	Rhoda	comedy	30
	Viva Valdez	comedy	30
	Rich Little	musical variety	60
	Phyllis	comedy	30
	Baseball	sports	150
	All in the Family	comedy	30
	Joe Forrester	crime drama	60
	Maude	comedy	30
	Medical Center	doctor series	60
	Jigsaw John	crime drama	60
Tuesday	I've Got a Secret	game	30
	Happy Days	comedy	30
	Movin' On	adventure	60
	Good Times	comedy	30
	Laverne and Shirley	comedy	30
	M A S H	comedy	30
	S.W.A.T.	crime drama	60
	Police Woman	crime drama	60
	One Day at a Time	comedy	30
	CBS Reports	news	60
	Rookies	crime drama	60
	NBC News Special	news	60

	PROGRAM TITLE	KIND OF PROGRAM	PROGRAM TIME (in minutes)
Wednesday	Jacksons	musical variety	30
	Bionic Woman	adventure	60
	Little House on the Prairie	western	120
	Kelly Montieth	comedy	30
	Cannon	crime drama	60
	Baretta	crime drama	60
	Blue Knight	crime drama	60
	Starsky and Hutch	crime drama	60
	Hawk	crime drama	60
Thursday	Waltons	family drama	60
	Welcome Back, Kotter	comedy	30
	Search for the Shinbara	adventure	60
	Barney Miller	comedy	30
	Hawaii Five – 0	crime drama	60
	Streets of San Francisco	crime drama	60
	Movie: "The Young Savages"	crime drama	120
	Barnaby Jones	crime drama	60
	Harry O	crime drama	60
Friday	Baseball game	sports	180
	Movie: "The Desperate Miles"	drama	90
	Sanford and Son	comedy	30
	The Practice	comedy	30
	Rockford Files	crime drama	60
	Movie: "Panic on the 5:22"	crime drama	90
	Police Story	crime drama	60

Task

a) Which of the programs are or were on German TV?

b) Which of the programs suggest aggression or violence?

c) Put the kinds of programs into a rank order showing the percentage (%) of program time in the week.

d) Make a similar list of programs and times for one week of German TV during prime time. Make a rank list as in c).

e) Compare lists. Which kind of program is given the most time on each list?

f) What kind of program do you like most? Why?

Language aids for your task reports	
a)	. . . was on German TV in . . . . . . is on our first/second/third . . . . . . is/was shown between . . . and . . . o'clock a.m./p.m.
b)	. . . sounds aggressive. . . . suggests . . . I think / suppose . . . has a lot of violence in it.
c)	. . . are given the most program time. ranks second/next/last. There are . . . programs than . . .
d)	I/We found . . . . . . films, ... films and . . . In the week . . . from . . . to . . . . . . films ranked . . . . .
e)	There are more . . . on US TV than on German TV. On American TV there are fewer . . . than in Germany. If the lists are typical there are fewer . . . on . . . TV than on . . . TV
f)	I like . . . best. I prefer . . . I watch . . . programs most. I never watch . . . I don't like/go for . . . . . . don't turn me on.

General opinions

- There should be | more / fewer | . . . programs on German TV.
- I don't understand why there shouldn't be | aggression / violence / war fighting / killings / fights / shooting | on TV.
- I don't mind . . . on TV.
- I find . . . . . . | bad / disgusting / terrible / bad for children / interesting / exciting / thrilling / fascinating / fantastic

An opinion poll

Write a questionnaire like this one in German, and ask people to answer it.

Which kind of program do you like best?

- ☐ crime dramas
- ☐ sports
- ☐ comedies
- ☐ family series
- ☐ westerns
- ☐ quiz shows
- ☐ musical shows

What do you like about criminal dramas:

- ☐ They are exciting, full of action.
- ☐ They are entertaining, like a puzzle or quiz.
- ☐ I like violence and aggression.
- ☐ I like it when the good guy wins against the bad guy.

What don't you like about crime dramas:

- ☐ It's cruel to show shooting and killing.
- ☐ I can't stand blood or dead bodies.
- ☐ It's too exciting, I can't sleep afterwards.
- ☐ It's boring; I don't know what it's all about.

Do you think children should watch crime on TV?

- ☐ No, they don't know the difference between a film and real life.
- ☐ No, they might come to think life is full of shooting and killing.
- ☐ No, they might come to think that it's wonderful to commit crimes.
- ☐ No, they get too excited, and that makes them ill.
- ☐ Yes, they know the difference between a film and real life.
- ☐ Yes, they forget the bad things or don't understand them.
- ☐ Yes, if they don't like it they can shut off the TV or go away.
- ☐ Yes, they should learn about criminals and violence.
- ☐ I don't know, I would like to get some more information first.
- ☐ I don't know, it's for the parents to decide.
- ☐ I don't know, I'm not interested in children or crime.

Perhaps you can think of some more questions.
Write a report about your findings.
Read it to your classmates.

5

Project 5

Focus on Germany

WunderAdventures in Germany

Germany is wunderbar—and now there's something even more wunderbar about it! Now there are exclusive programs for the individual traveller who is adventurous and appreciates comfort and convenience, too. Wunder-Adventures are special-interest programs for small groups. They include the two following unique and enchanting tours which enable them to see Germany as the conventional traveller never can.

The Wunderbike Tour

The group bikes through the Upper Rhine Valley and Black Forest on specially-designed touring bicycles, at an easy pace of twenty-five to thirty miles per day, accompanied by one biking tour director and one guide driving a van with a bike trailer for luggage. The van can also be used in bad weather. Tour price is $725 per person MAP, double occupancy, plus airfare.

The Wunderbuggy Tour

This is a romantic tour by stagecoach or Landau wagon through Upper Bavaria. The group visits famous landmarks like the Wies Church and Neuschwanstein Castle. Tour price is $1,139 per person, double occupancy, including all meals, plus airfare.

By bus, by tram, by S-train.

Going by bus, tram or S-train is quite easy, fast and comfortable; so is going by underground. But it isn't cheap, and before you know it you have spent most of your money on fares.

Never get on a bus or train without a valid ticket. If you get caught without a ticket or with a ticket which doesn't cover the whole distance there will be heavy fines from DM 20,– to DM 150,–.

If you go the same route often the best thing is to buy a weekly or monthly ticket which is cheaper than individual tickets.

Bus and tram systems are different from city to city. Usually you can get a very neat description of them in English at the information office.

5

Project 5

Focus on other countries

A personal note of a Southern Irish Protestant

On the surface, there is no real difference between myself and my Catholic neighbours at home in "Canburry", Dublin, yet we are aware of our differences. As a young girl I rarely played with Catholic children, and my education and social life was almost entirely confined to the small "Protestant community" around me. Catholics didn't come to my birthday party and I didn't come to theirs. In short, we Protestants of the south are Irish, but Irish with a difference.
"Of the Irish Nation, but not of the people"
(Conor Cruise O'Brian, The States of Ireland, Penguin 1974, p. 25)

The Northern Ireland (Ulster) conflict

You know that Ulster is a part of the United Kingdom, and you also know that in Northern Ireland some young Catholics fight and kill young Protestants and vice versa.

Why is this terrible fight going on? Why do British people fight British people? Why the terror? Who started it, and how did it start?

Here is a brief summary of the Irish Conflict. Of course, it is impossible to give the whole complicated background. But maybe you can ask your history teacher for more detailed information.

From the Irish history

1171

English troops land in Ireland. A lot of Irish noblemen lose their land. The King of England makes himself "Lord of Ireland". English settlers come to Ireland.

1500 until 1700

The Anglo-Irish begin to hate the English rule and rise against it: rebellion. The Irish noblemen get support from the Spanish fleet.
English kings and queens send more settlers to colonize Ireland.

1649

Cromwell invades Ireland to beat Irish and Anglo-Irish rebels. They call it the anti-Catholic crusades. Cromwell gives land to his supporters and veterans.

1690

William of Orange beats Catholic James II. He sees to it that Protestants rule Ireland. They own the land but often live in England.

1690–1760

Protestant rule over Ireland established.

1794

During French-English war the Society of the United Irishmen sympathizes with the French Revolution. They have to go underground.

end of 17th century

While England's economy is going up Ireland's economy cannot develop; it produces just enough to feed people and send raw materials to England.

1795

A counter-revolutionary group, the Orange Order, named after the Protestant William of Orange, is formed.

1845

Potato pest in Ireland: the Great Famine. Years of hunger and starvation in Ireland. A lot of Irish go to America.

1916 until 1918

1916 Easter Rising in Dublin, street fights. 15 Irish leaders shot. Sinn Fein movement becomes stronger. 1918 Sinn Fein Party wins all Irish seats in Parliament.

1949

Eire leaves the British Commonwealth and becomes a republic.

1937

Southern Ireland becomes an independent republic with a new constitution.

autumn 1968

Civil Rights Movement starts peaceful demonstrations in Ulster.
(October 1977 Nobel Peace Prize for Irish Women Peace Movement.)

1969

In Northern Ireland attack by Orange crowds on Catholic ghettoes in Belfast. 9 people killed, 500 houses burnt. British troops stop it.

August 9th 1971

300 people arrested in Ulster without trial.

January 30th 1972

Bloody Sunday: 13 civilians in peaceful demonstration killed by British troops.
July 1972: IRA cease fire breaks down.

5

Project 5

Language study package

MINI MODEL TEXTS

I am not aggressive. If I found someone stealing apples from our trees I would not phone the police, but I would tell him or her to go away and keep as many as he or she likes. If my friend came late for a date I would say, "No problem. I have plenty of time". And if someone stepped on my foot on a bus I would say, "I hope you are feeling fine on my foot." If I had to be reborn as an animal I would love to be a dog. I would eat dog bisquits and sleep in my own bed.

One day **a bank robber** walked towards a bank. As he was very nervous he did not see father's son who was playing in front of the bank and knocked him over. The little son cried and told his father what had happened. Father was furious. He went into the bank and then he pointed at the robber who was holding two guns in his hands. Father took the robber by the shoulder and knocked him down. The bank clerks were very happy and carried father and son on their shoulders while the police was aresting the robber. They told the reporters that father had knocked the robber down.

WORDS

It's	right	to fight	people
It isn't	wrong	to steal	children
	a crime	to kill	animals
	bad	to hurt	friends
	good	to help	things
	against the law	to stand by	policemen
		to get angry at	criminals
		to laugh with	parents
		to laugh at	teachers
		to beat	pupils
		to shout at	. . .
		. . .	

Now change your sentences like this:

. . .ing	is	right.
	isn't	wrong.
		. . .

Word study

Chambers Universal Learners' Dictionary is a very good word book. Study the examples and explanations it gives for some words that you have seen and used in this project so far.

brutal *adj* very cruel or severe: *She received a brutal beating; His treatment of her was brutal.*

furious *adj* **1** very angry: *She was furious with him about it; in a furious mood.*
2 violent: *a furious argument; a furious storm; The motorcyclist drove a furious speed.*

aggressive *adj* ready to attack or oppose; quarrelsome: *a most aggressive boy; That child is so aggressive that he is always fighting at school; He is not aggressive enough to succeed in business.*

reckless *adj* very careless; acting or done without any thought of the consequences: *a reckless driver, reckless driving; He is very reckless when he is drunk; He dashed out, reckless of the danger.*

rough *adj* **1** not smooth: *Her skin felt rough.*
2 uneven: *a rough path.* **3** harsh, unpleasant: *a rough voice.* **4** noisy and violent: *His behaviour was very rough.*

irate *adj* angry: *The irate butcher chased the thieving dog out of the shop; I became more and more irate as I waited for my friend who was very late in arriving.*

angry *adj* feeling or showing anger: *He was so angry that he was unable to speak; He regretted his angry words; He gets angry over nothing; She got angry at the children and hit them; The sky looks angry – it is going to rain.*

violent *adj* **1** having, using, or showing great force: *There was a violent storm at sea; a violent earthquake; He was usually drunk and often violent; He has a violent temper.* **2** caused by force: *a violent death.*

raging *adj* **1** violent: *a raging storm.* **2** very painful or extreme: *a raging toothache; a raging fever.*

rowdy *adj* noisy and rough: *rowdy children, rowdy behaviour; Their party became more and more rowdy.*

rude *adj* **1** not polite; showing bad manners: *rude children, rude behaviour; Don't be rude (to me)!*
2 roughly made: *They built a rude shelter.* **3** sudden: *a rude awakening; a rude surprise.*

Which of the examples tell you best what the words mean?

Using language to retell what someone said

Do you remember what Georgia said?

A	Georgia:	"I **am** in ninth grade."
B	Georgia said to the interviewer	that she **was** in ninth grade.
A	Georgia:	"**I do** my homework in the study period."
B	Georgia told the interviewer	that she **did** her homework in the study period.
A	Georgia:	"In the evening we **have** dinner with our parents."
B	Georgia remarked	that in the evening they **had** dinner with their parents.
	reporting clause	reported clause

Verben, die in der direkten Rede in der Gegenwart stehen, stehen in der indirekten Rede in der Vergangenheit.

Reported speech: practice

Change these sentences from direct speech to reported speech.

The boy said to his father,	"I have invented a bubble gun. I will make a lot of money with it. I'm going to make a million dollars."
The boy wrote in his letter,	"I have gone to sell my invention. Dad only laughed at me. I took some stuff for sandwiches."
The boy's mother said,	"You have driven the boy from his home. He will starve. He is just a baby."
Peter told his friend,	"I love violence on TV. I always watch detective films. I hate all bad men. I want to join the police after school. I will fight violence and crime."
Carol said to the interviewer,	"I liked The Waltons best. I have watched only a few criminal films. I found sports shows boring. I have seen all the quiz shows. I will watch the new western series tomorrow."

reporting clause: past tense — She **said** (that)

direct speech	reported speech
present tense "I do my homework."	past tense . . . (that) she did her homework.
present perfect "We have never learnt German."	past perfect . . . (that) they had never learnt German.
past tense "Yesterday I helped my friend."	past perfect . . . (that) he had helped his friend.
will-future "I will use the money for a party."	conditional I . . . (that) he would use he money for a party.

Using the bare infinitive

Fill in the missing verbs:

Dear Loretta

Can you .[1]. . next weekend with me? Mother and Dad are going to visit some friends in Lexington and they would .[2]. . me with them, but I don't want to go. My grandmother could .[3]. ., but it would .[4]. . more fun, if you came. I should .[5]. . alone, but you know my parents! You needn't .[6]. . though – Janie and Carol are coming over on Saturday – we won't .[7]. . bored. Ask your parents and I'll .[8]. . you on Thursday night. O.K.?

Your cousin,
Martha

P.S. We can .[9]. . you at the bus station.

spend	be	be
take	stay	call
come	worry	meet

Make + object + bare infinitive

The English **made** the Irish noblemen leave the country.
The Protestant landowners **made** the Irish farmers pay rents.

Write sentences with **made:**

My parents	me	leave	home	at six	made
His funny stories	everybody	laugh			made
Our Maths teacher	work hard	us			made

Let + object + bare infinitive

During the Great Famine the British authorities **let** thousands of Irish leave the country.
The judge **let** the gang leader go free.
A lot of parents aren't **letting** their children stay out in the evenings.

Write sentences with **let:**

My friend	use	his bicycle		let
My parents	stay out	until 11 p.m.		let
Our English teacher	us	use a dictionary	doing tests	let

6

Project 6

Starters

Magic dreams

We begin – can you go on?

- Last night I found out that I could walk through walls.
- Last night I woke up in the middle of the night and saw a flying saucer coming down on me.
- This morning I woke up and found myself sitting on top of the Empire State Building.
- My dog has become very strange. He opens the fridge in the kitchen, but never takes anything out.
- When I took my breakfast apple out this morning it had the face of my maths teacher. That must be magic.

These are the opening lines for some stories you might invent. Use your imagination!

6

① Flying saucers and little green men?

Project 6

Strange things

– 3.00 p.m., June 24, 1947, Washington State, U.S.A.

Kenneth Arnold was flying his plane over the Cascade Mountains when he saw nine round shining objects flying near him. They were all about as big as his plane. By checking their position at different times he found that they were flying at about 2,700 km per hour – much faster than any plane in 1947!
Arnold later told a reporter, "Each one went up and down as it moved, like a saucer when you throw it along the water."

– 2.00 p.m., January 7, 1948, Kentucky, U.S.A.

Many people reported seeing a strange flying object. There were no planes near there at the time. The object was round and about 90 metres across.
At 2.30 p.m. three fighter planes were sent to investigate.
At 2.45 Captain Mantell, one of the pilots saw the object. His last radio report was, "It's still above me but I'm getting closer. I'm going up to 6,000 metres."
Then he lost radio contact.
At 3.50 the object disappeared. A few minutes later a report arrived. Mantell's plane had crashed and he was dead.

– U.S.A., 1967

A UFO was seen by people in eleven different towns over a period of four days. The UFO was about 8 metres across, round and glowing. It changed colour and followed people and cars.
One policeman reported, "It was so bright that we could read our watches in the police car at night."

Lots of reports like these are made each year. The usual description: a round, glowing object, travelling very fast. Some people think that these UFOs are spaceships from other planets. Scientists have simpler explantions. They say that what people usually see are weather balloons or birds or stars or planes. The atmosphere of the Earth can play tricks on our eyes.
Scientists investigating UFO reports usually find that the people have only seen the UFO for a short time. They can't answer the three important questions:

- How big was it?
- How far away was it?
- How fast was it going?

because:

- An object that looks big and far away may really be little and near.
- An object that you think is far away and moving fast may really be near and moving slowly.
- An object that seems to be following you may be far away and not moving at all.

If you don't believe this, walk through a forest on a moonlight night. You will think that the moon is following you.
What the people in the eleven U.S. towns saw in 1967 was really just the planet Venus!

Put it in writing

Draw the following summary grid in your exercise-book.
Then fill in the words and write a short text.

Kenneth Arnold	was	saw	checked	found	was	went	told
	flying						
	surprised						
It						was	
There	were						
The UFOs		were	had	went	looked		were
	nine flying objects	round	the shape of . . .	up . . .		in . . .	going faster . . .
		flying near . . .				on . . .	
		flying at . . .				at . . .	

2 Interviews

When I was in the United States in 1952/53 I went by train from Holland, Michigan, to Ann Arbor, Michigan. After a farewell party the night before I was very sleepy, closed my eyes and dozed off a little. Suddenly someone gave me a pat on the shoulder and asked me, "Do you believe in flying saucers?" I quickly answered, "I've never seen one. So I don't believe there are flying saucers." The man said, "This, ladies and gentlemen, brings our score to 9 : 2. Nine who believe and two who don't." I was a bit surprised. Who was he talking to? Then I noticed he had a microphone in his hand. He explained that there was a transmitter on the train and that we were 'on the air'.

Why don't you make up such interviews? It is a good language training and it can be great fun, too.

Some questions the interviewers could ask:

– Have you Has anyone	ever seen a flying saucer?
– Do you Does anyone	believe in flying saucers or other UFOs?

– Any idea where they come from?

– Why do you think they come near our planet?

– If you don't believe in manned flying saucers what else could the flying objects be?

– What would they do if they landed on Earth?

Your classmates might play the roles of people you are going to interview.

Possible roles

A

You are a UFO fanatic. You live on the coast of Wales. You watch out for UFOs most of your time. You have a radioscope and you are in touch with the UFO crews. They have visited you. They are very good-looking, about 1.30 metres tall, have blue skin and yellow eyes. They speak English with a German accent.

B

You are a lorry driver. On one of your trips to Scotland you saw six shining silver discs in the sky. You stopped your lorry and walked up to the top of a hill. You saw the six space ships land. Little yellow men left the spacecraft and used laser beam guns to shoot a herd of sheep. They carried the animals into the ship.

C

You are a LUFTHANSA flight captain (a pilot). You fly a DC 10. You have been a pilot for 14 years. You have never seen a flying saucer. But you have met a lot of people who claim to have seen UFOs and actually talked to men from outer space.

D

You are the Scottish shepherd whose herd of sheep was carried away by the spacemen. When the ships landed you and your two dogs hid behind a rock. You don't think the sheep were killed. You were surprised to see how strong the little men were. They did not speak.

E

You are yourself.
Answer the interview questions as you like. Explain that your English is not perfect and that you are sorry to make so many mistakes. Don't forget to tell the interviewer all about yourself.

F

You were out on your bike one day. It was late and it was getting dark. You had your headlight on. Suddenly your lamp burst. Then you saw a silver beam of light. You felt hot. Your head felt as if it was filled with hot boiling water. The last thing you remember was a strange noise.

G

You are an icecream man with a van. You were on your way home. It had been a cold day, so you had not sold much of your icecream. Suddenly you had the feeling that there was a large cloud above your car and you heard a humming noise. Suddenly your van was in the focus of strong light. You stopped and jumped out. You saw the UFO.

H

You are the interviewer. You ask all your guests to answer your questions and tell their stories. You have two assistants who write down notes to remember and retell the stories.

I

You are the interviewer's assistant. Write down notes and retell the stories later.

J

See I.

K

Your were in the cellar of your home to fetch some potatoes. There was no light, so you had to feel your way to the potato box. Suddenly there was a very strong blue light outside shining through the small window. All of a sudden a terrible face was at the window staring at you: a big mouth with silvery teeth, three small eyes, no nose. You screamed. The light went out. You heard a horrible noise.

L

You were alone in the swimming pool of your house. You were floating on your back. You saw a silver cloud. Suddenly the cloud took the shape of a flying saucer. You waved your hand at the spacecraft. It came down quickly and stopped in the air about 10 metres above your head. A small door opened and a ladder was pushed down. A beautiful girl came down. With a smile she gave you a bottle of POOLAROMA and climbed up the ladder again.

M

You are an electronics fan. The other day you had built an electronic receiver transmitter unit. Through your earphone you heard strange noises. You tried to establish communication. You cried, "Who are you? Give me your code number. Can't you speak English?" Then the answer came in perfect English, "If you want to stay alive destroy your transmitter receiver. This is the Mars destroyer unit SEX 707." You destroyed your machine at once.

N

You were fishing at a big pond near your home. Suddenly a huge UFO appeared and began to descend on your pond. As it came nearer it became smaller and smaller. As it touched the water it was no bigger than a button. It sank. A fish gobbled it up. You caught that fish. Inside the fish you found the flying saucer. You took the find to the Secret Service.

Task Make up more UFO stories.

Perhaps you could make an interview with Noah or the American ark people. (See page 109.)

3

				9 miracles
		2 amulets	5 angels	10 ghosts
Do you believe in	1 horoscopes	3 wonder doctors	6 demons	11 flying saucers
		4 talismans	7 black days	12 little men from outer space
			8 mind reading	13 the evil eyes
				14 telepathy

?

Which is what?

a) The prediction of the future of a person based on the position of the stars and planets at the time of his or her birth.

b) A spirit, usually of a dead person, that appears or is heard after midnight.

c) Something that we cannot make happen and/or explain.

d) A spirit with a message from God.

e) An object which people believe has magic powers to protect the owner.

f) The same as e.

g) Days full of bad luck for a person.

h) The power of making someone ill or miserable by just looking at him/her.

i) A flying object that looks like a saucer or disc.

j) Small creatures that come from other stars.

k) Sometimes called quack doctors. They lay their hands on you to cure the illness.

l) Devils, evil spirits from Hell.

m) Understanding what goes on in another person's mind.

n) Understanding what goes on in another person's mind without talking with him, and without seeing him.

4 A passage from the bible

And God said unto Noah: . . .
Make thee an ark of wood;
rooms shalt thou make in the ark . . .
A window shalt thou make to the ark . . .
and the door of the ark
shalt thou let in the side . . .

And of every living thing . . .,
two of every sort
shalt thou bring into the ark,
to keep them alive with thee;
they shall be male and female.

And Noah went in, and his sons,
and his wife, and his sons' wives . . .
because of the waters of the flood.

And the flood was forty days
upon the earth . . .
and all the high hills . . . were covered.

thee = you
thou = you
shalt = shall

Another ark

The ark in this picture looks like Noah's Ark.

This ark was built before 1947 by people in Washington Mud Flats. They believed that in 1947 a second flood would kill all creatures on Earth. They put everything in the ark that they wanted to save for a new life after the flood. They had a full orchestra in the ark. But the flood did not come.

Think and talk about the reading passage

- Do you know any other objects that people built or made?
- Have you ever built or made something that showed what you had in your mind?
- We all have feelings. We have them and we need them to be in contact with and understand the people and the world around us. And we all believe in things that we cannot understand and explain.

What makes people do things like building an ark?

1 fear	**2** craziness	**3** publicity	**4** survival instinct
5 do-it-yourself fun	**6** belief in God	**7** a voice in their hearts	**8** play instinct
9 hobby	**10** showing off	**11** attracting tourists	**12** too much free time
13 too much money	**14** unhappiness	**15** creativity	**16** . . .

Language aids

I don't know what . . . . . means.
What's the meaning of . . . . .?
Can you explain what . . . . is?
I think it's . . . . that makes people . . . . .
I believe it's a case of . . . . . .?
I know someone who . . . . .
I once watched a film on TV . . . .

Ask your classmates. Make a complete opinion poll.

Two spirituals

Didn't it rain

Didn't it rain, little children, my Lord.
Didn't it rain, little children, my Lord.

It rained forty days, forty nights without a stopping,
Noah was there when the rain started dropping,
he was so busy, 'cause the rain wasn't stopping,
and he couldn't hear the angels when they moaned.

It rained forty days, forty nights, you couldn't see,
some climbed the mountains and some climbed the tree,
some were busy rowing, shouting: Noah, rescue me!
But he couldn't hear the angels when they moaned.

Now the people they were going from door to door
crying: Old Noah, why don't you take some more?
But he had the windows closed, so they beat on the door.
And he couldn't hear the angels when they moaned.

Get on board, little children

Get on board, little children,
get on board, little children,
there's room for many more.

The Gospel train is coming,
I hear it just at hand,
I hear the car wheels moving
and rumbling through the land.

Get on board, little children,
get on board, little children,
get on board, little children,
there's room for many more.

The fare is cheap, and all can go,
the rich and poor are there,
no second class aboard this train,
no difference in the fare.

Get on board, little children,
get on board, little children,
get on board, little children,
there's room for many more.

Get organized

Can you discuss and answer these questions?

- Why did Noah not open the windows and doors?
- Why does the song writer make the singers ask: Didn't it rain?
- Can you understand why Russian and British expeditions set out to look for Noah's Ark on Mount Ararat?
- What is behind the story of the great flood? Has it perhaps something to do with earthquakes?
- What is the Gospel train?
- Where does it go?
- Why is there no second class?
- How much is the fare (the ticket)?
- Who are the 'little children'?
- What can the writers of the songs have had in mind when they wrote the two texts?
- What do the two texts mean to you?
- What have they to do with our project on the supernatural?

5 Borley rectory: Britain's most haunted house

The legends

Long before Borley Rectory was built
there was a monastery in that place.
A monk from there fell in love
with a nun from a nearby nunnery
(possibly from Bures, about 8 miles away).
They tried to escape together in a coach
but they were caught.
The monk was hanged
and the nun walled up alive.
Since that time people have often claimed
to have seen the ghost of a sad looking nun.
Some say they have seen a phantom coach
racing along the old road through Borley.

Others say that a French nun was
kidnapped from the nunnery
at Bures by a member of the
Waldgrave family (the owners of Borley
Manor). He murdered her at the place
where Borley Rectory was later built.

The Bull family and Borley Rectory

The Reverend Henry Bull was vicar at Borley Church from 1862 until his death in 1892. In 1863 he built Borley Rectory for his large family. It was a dark, gloomy building and almost from the beginning strange things happened there. The nun's ghost was said to appear frequently, especially on the 28th of July.

The Bulls knew about the stories but did not speak about them in front of their children. One friend of the family tells how the Reverend Bull had a window bricked up because the nun often appeared outside it. Guests were asked to lunch or tea but never to dinner.

On one occasion, on the 28th of July, 1901, four of the Bull daughters saw the nun gliding along Nun's Walk in daylight. Sometimes the figure of a man was seen in the passages of the house and strange music was heard.

In 1892 the Reverend Henry Bull died and his son, Henry "Harry" Bull took his position. The hauntings continued.

Do you believe these reports?

If you don't believe the reports, then try and suggest other explanations.

Some other Borley experiences

Miss Meg Barton, daughter of the church warden at Borley

"While I was riding my pony, I saw a figure about five feet tall and wearing long robes. I said, 'Good afternoon', but she never looked up and I thought, 'What a rude person'. My pony shied and snorted and when I looked back, the figure was gone."

A local doctor's wife

"It was a foggy evening and I was driving along a lane when I saw a nun walking along. I thought it was a bit strange for her to be out so late so I stopped to give her a lift. She stopped, looked into the car for a second and then just disappeared into thin air."

Edward Cooper, occupant of the Priory Cottage for many years

"One night I looked out of the window and saw an old-fashioned coach and horses standing in the yard. It was moonlight and I could see one or two people sitting on the box seat. I called my wife but when she got there, it had just disappeared. Later on we found out that the old coach road used to run right by the house here."

Gordon Dobbs*

London Veterinary

"I saw a figure walking across the path in front of me. I was about to call out a greeting when I realized that it made no sound, nor did it disturb the puddles of water over which it passed. I knew of the legend and when I realized that the figure was that of a nun, my heart froze . . . I wondered what a nun was doing strolling around at that time of night . . . untill I realized it was not a human figure in front of us. One moment it was there. The next it was gone. It could only have been a ghost."

* Gordon Dobbs did not come from Borley and researchers were never able to find him to confirm this report.

Get organized

What things have been seen and heard?
Make a list.
Use the headings:
Who? What? Where? When?

6 Some fables first told by Aesop

in the sixth century before Christ.

The quack frog

Once upon a time a frog left his home and told the world that he was a doctor who knew all about drugs and cures and that he could do away with all diseases. A fox heard him talk.

He called out, "You a doctor! How can you promise to heal others when you cannot cure yourself? Look at your lame legs and your face."

Moral: Doctor heal yourself.

Jupiter and the tortoise

Jupiter was about to marry. He invited all the animals to a banquet.

They all came except the tortoise. Jupiter was much surprised. When he met the tortoise later he asked him why he had not come to the banquet.

The tortoise said, "I don't like parties. There's no place like home."
Jupiter was very angry.

He shouted, "From now on you will carry your house on your back. That way you will never get away from home."

Hercules and Minerva

Hercules was once travelling along a road when he saw an apple lying in his way. He stepped on it with his foot. The apple did not crush but it doubled in size. He kicked it and used his stick to beat it. But it could not be smashed. It grew larger and larger. Hercules felt helpless and threw away his stick.

Just then Minerva was passing by. She told him, "Leave that apple alone. It is the apple of discord. If you leave it as it is, it will remain small. But if you become violent and angry it will swell up into the thing you see before you.

The wasp and the snake

A wasp was sitting on a snake's head. It stung him several times. And it stayed there and laughed at the snake. The snake was furious and tried to get rid of the wasp. But nothing worked. At last he said, "I will kill you – even at the cost of my life."

And he put his head under the wheel of a passing waggon. They both died.

Task Divide into small groups.
choose one of the fables for reading.
Tell your classmates about the contents.

- You may not believe in Greek and Roman gods and you know that animals can't speak. But can you explain why the texts are nevertheless interesting and meaningful?
- Choose one of the fables and learn it by heart.

6

Project 6

Focus on Germany

Doctors and dentists

Anything wrong with your teeth? Any health problem? No problem in Germany. You can choose your doctor yourself. To make safe, however, ask a German before you contact a dentist or doctor because some of them are extremely busy, and the office will put you on a long waiting list.

When you have found a dentist or doctor, phone his or her office and make an appointment.

If you need a doctor at night in a case of emergency or over the weekend, call the emergency service („ärztlicher Notdienst"). Any police station, the local Red Cross or the local newspapers will tell you the emergency service phone number.

On Sundays and at nights certain chemist's shops (pharmacies) are open on demand. They take turns. All chemist's shops have notice boards indicating which pharmacies are open all day and all night (geöffnet, offen, Nachtdienst).

You will have to pay the doctor if your parents have a private insurance that covers the expenses later. It is advisable to have a special holiday insurance, just in case!

A German pharmacy

A British chemist's shop

6

Project 6

Focus on other countries

India

Official Name:	Bharat, Republic of India
Government:	federal republic
Capital City:	New Delhi
Official Languages:	Hindi, English (semi-official)
Official Religion:	None
Area:	3,268,090 sq. km.
Population:	approximately: 654,000,000
Religious groups:	Hindu 82.7%, Moslem 11.2%, Christian 2.6%, Sikh 1.9%, Buddhist 0.7%, Jain 0.5%, other 0.4%
Language groups:	Assamese 1.9%, Bengali 9.5%, Gujurati 5.4%, Hindi 34%, Kanada 4.6%, Malayalam 8.1%, Marathi 8.1%, Oriya 4.2%, Punjabi 3.4%, Sindhi 0.4%, Tamil 8%, Telugu 9.4%, Urdu 6%, Kashmiri 0.5%

In the preceding unit you learned that one of India's main problems is how to feed its people. But India has a lot more problems:

The caste system in India

One aspect of India which Europeans find very difficult to understand is the caste system. Traditionally, all Indians belonged to one of five groups. These were, in order of importance:

- Brahmins: priests
- Kshatriyas: soldiers and kings
- Vaishyas: traders and merchants
- Shudras: skilled workers
- Pariahs: unskilled workers, the so-called "untouchables".

The untouchable caste are now called "Harijans" meaning "children of God".

Mahatma Ghandi began trying to break down the barriers between the castes in the 1930s and the system was abolished by law after independence in 1947. Despite this, many Indians still only marry within their own caste and group and still only do particular jobs.

India – a developing country?

Europeans think of India as a developing country and do not know that there has been heavy industry there since the end of the 19th century and atomic power plants since the beginning of the 1960s.
Find out what you can about heavy industry in India. Particularly interesting is the iron and steel industry and the work of its founder, Jamsetji Tata (1839–1904).

How British is India?

India is a member of the Commonwealth. This seems a bit strange when you think that the British occupied India with an army for more than a hundred years. An Indian journalist, interviewed by the CONTACTS team, explained it in this way:
"We don't think of ourselves as British at all, but many of our important men admired the British and their institutions, for example, the legal system. We also admire the British idea of fair play, even if they didn't play very fair with us."

Find out what you can about the British influence on modern India. What is the meaning of "being a member of the Commonwealth"?

6

Project 6

Language study package

MINI MODEL TEXTS

UFO. I was out on my bike the other day. Suddenly I noticed something shining in the sky. Then I saw two more shining objects. I jumped off my bike and went behind a tree. The three flying objects came down quickly and landed not far from where I was. The objects were round and no bigger than a small car. The door of one of the objects opened and twelve little yellow men came out. They went to my bike and took it to pieces. They went back with the parts of my bike in thin little yellow hands. They went inside and soon the three UFOs took off. When I looked at the place where they had taken my bike to pieces I found a note saying "Thank you".

This morning I woke up **in hospital** with a terrible headache. I remembered what had happened the night before. I was out on my bike. It was late and it was getting dark. I had my new headlight on. Suddenly my lamp burst with a strange noise. Then I saw the silver beam of light coming from above. I felt very hot. I thought my head was filled with boiling water. That is the last thing I can remember. Now I feel as if my head is filled with cold water. I cannot speak and I cannot walk. But I can write. And my English is much better than before. The next beam should be a maths beam.

WORDS

Strange people	came	here	and	went . . .
A strange object	went	there		touched . . .
	followed a man	nowhere		disappeared . . .
	landed	to his house		rattled . . .
	talked to me	in a field		kicked . . .
	was built	at his car		swept . . .
		behind some trees		shouted at . . .
		over the water		cried . . .
		by Noah and his sons		wept . . .
		by some people near New York		crashed into . . .
		near me		grinned at . . .
		up to me		lifted . . .

The time/tense aspect.

present tense	Most Jamaicans	speak	English	English	is spoken	by most Jamaiscans
present perfect	No boy	has ever made	a bubble gun	A bubble gun	has never been made	(doer not important)
past tense	A boy	invented	the bubble gun	The bubble gun	was invented	by a boy
future time	Someone	will invent	a space bike (one day)	(One day) a space bike	will be invented	(doer not) known)
	THE DOER		THE OBJECT	THE SUBJECT		THE DOER

A horror castle

Change these sentences into the passive.

At the gate the guards will stop you. They will search you from top to bottom. They will ask you lots of questions. They will give you a passport and a golden key. They will open the gate for you. A beautiful princess will welcome you. She will show you your bedroom. Later a servant will call you to dinner. They will serve you the most fantastic meals and your favourite sweets. At half past ten the servants will take you to your room. At midnight ghosts will wake you up. They will kick dead men's skulls around. They will ask you to be the referee in a footskull match. They will invite you to make music with them. They will tell you to beat the drum with two bones with hands on them. They will pay you gold for that.	You will be stopped at . . . . . . searched . . . . . .

Tell this story in the past tense of both active and passive voice.

At the gate the guards stopped me.	I was stopped by . . . at . . . . . .

7 Survival

Project 7

Starters

Scale of Survival Needs

absolutely necessary

helpful and useful

useful in some situations, but not necessary

nice to have, but not necessary

unnecessary

entertainment
euro cup
sports
water
warmth
tools
food
THE COMPLETE WORKS OF WILLIAM SHAKESPEARE
THE LORD OF THE RINGS
money
THE COMPLETE POEMS AND PLAYS OF TS ELIOT
BRISTOL-MYERS
Extra-Strength
Aspirin Pain Reliever
COPE
free time
medicine

Get organized

- Look at the items in the collage.
  Which of them are

  A: absolutely necessary to survive,

  B: helpful and useful

  C: useful in some situations, but not necessary

  D: nice to have, but not necessary

  E: absolutely unnecessary to stay alive?

- Then make a scale of the items starting with the most important one and ending with the least important one.
  Perhaps you can think of items that are not in the collage.
- Compare your scale with that of your classmates.
  Explain why you arranged your scale in the way you did.
- Now make up two lists:

physical needs (for your body)	**psychological needs** (for your soul)

- Experts say that only **four things** are necessary for physical survival:

  w . . . ., f . . ., sh . . . . ., c . . . . . .

  Can you name them?

  Where did you put them on your scale?

Task Please, explain the precautions shown on the next page.

never don't	use . . . stay . . . . seek . . . . touch	
. . . . .	is provides	a good shelter

The best thing is to . . . . . .

During a . . . . are no good . . . . .

Have you ever been outside in a thunderstorm?

When? How was it? What did you do?

Survival precautions

during a thunderstorm

If there is no other shelter

keep away from

small sheds
or huts

towers

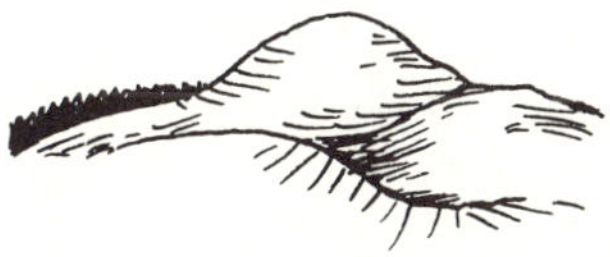

wire-fences

hilltops

pylons

SEEK SHELTER

in woods with
trees of similar size

at the foot of an
overhanging cliff

in hollows
in the ground

If there is only one tree
in an open space seek shelter
there, but keep away from
it, never touch it or its roots.

7

Project 7

Survival

❶ The world's largest cities
population 1981

Mexico City, Mexico	13.75 millions
Shanghai, China	12.00 millions
Sao Paulo, Brazil	11.23 millions
New York, U.S.A.	9.22 millions
Tokyo, Japan	9.03 millions
Peking, China	9.02 millions
Moscow, U.S.S.R.	7.91 millions
Los Angeles, U.S.A.	7.08 millions
Chicago, U.S.A.	7.03 millions
London, England	7.03 millions
Paris, France	6.97 millions
Seoul, South Korea	6.88 millions
Bombay, India	5.97 millions
Buenos Aires, Argentina	5.83 millions
Calcutta, India	5.35 millions
Cairo, Egypt	5.10 millions
Rio de Janeiro, Brazil	5.09 millions
Philadelphia, U.S.A.	4.77 millions
Jakarta, Indonesia	4.58 millions
Hongkong, Hongkong	4.51 millions

Task Look the cities up in your atlas.
Then look at the drawing on the next page
and check which climate zone each city belongs to.
Which climate zone has the most big cities? Which the fewest?

Some of the largest cities are
in the poorest countries of the world.
Most of the large third world cities
have slums.

It is hard to survive in the country:
The poor people have no jobs
or they have to work for a few
coins in large plantations.
So the young people go to the
cities, try to make a living,
and end up in slums.

The Climate Zones

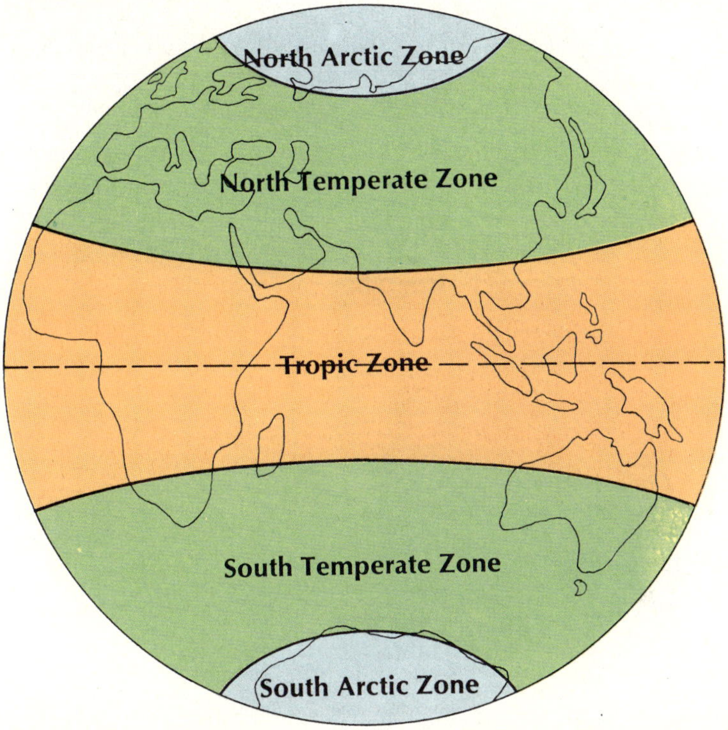

CLIMATE ZONES	CONDITIONS / CHARACTERISTICS	MEANS OF MAKING A LIVING
TROPIC	DESERT – hot, dry; extremely cold nights	
	SAVANNAH – one or two rainy periods; humid, warm	sheep, cattle
	RAIN FOREST – hot, humid; no change of seasons	tropical farming, coffee, tea
NORTH AND SOUTH TEMPERATE	PINE FOREST – 4 months summer; cold winter with snow	fishing; some farming and livestock; industry
	DECIDUOUS FOREST – more than 4 months summer; warm winter with rain	industry; livestock and farming
	STEPPE – hot summer, more than 4 months; cold, dry winter	
ARCTIC	TUNDRA – short, cold summer with midnight sun; long winter, permanent frost	animal fur, fishing

2

HUNGER IS ALL SHE HAS EVER KNOWN

Margaret was found in a back lane of Calcutta, lying in a doorway, unconscious from hunger. Inside, her mother had just died in childbirth.

Meanwhile, in America we eat 4.66 pounds of food a day per person, then throw away enough to feed a family of six in India.

But Margaret's story can have a happy ending, because she has a CCF sponsor now. And for only $ 12 a month you can also sponsor a child like Margaret and help provide food, clothing, shelter – and love.

You will receive the child's picture, personal history, and the opportunity to exchange letters, Christmas cards – and priceless friendship.

Since 1938, American sponsors have found this to be an intimate, person-to-person way of sharing their blessings with youngsters around the world.

So won't you help? Today?

Sponsors are urgently needed this month for children in: India, Brazil, Philippines, Indonesia and Guatemala. (Or let us select a child for you from our emergency list.)

CHRISTIAN CHILDREN'S FUND, Inc.

Box 26511, Richmond, Va. 23261

I wish to sponsor a ☐ boy ☐ girl

in (Country) __________

☐ Choose a child who needs me most. I will pay $ 12 a month. Send me child's name, story, address and picture.

☐ I cannot sponsor a child but want to give $ __________

My name and address: __________

Tasks

lane – a small street
sponsor – someone who gives money
blessing – good fortune

Language aids

Read the advertisement again.

a) Does Margaret have the four basic things she needs to survive?

b) What kind of survival needs is the advertisement talking about?

c) Which needs for survival can a sponsor give Margaret?

d) Which needs can a sponsor not meet?

❸ Nowhere to call home

outside,	Tonight, thousands of young people,
not comfortable	2,000 of them girls,
	will be sleeping rough
	on the streets of London.
	As bitter cold of winter
	blows round them
	they will keep warm
	by walking,
	finally settling down
	in a shop-doorway,
	a park bench or railway station
broken, interrupted	for a fitful sleep.
	The story of 22-year-old Janice
	is typical.
	She had just arrived
a cheap hotel	at a hostel in North Kensington
for young travellers	when I spoke to her.
	After months of sleeping rough
	she had spent her first night in a bed
	she could call her own.
	This is her story:
do not live together	My parents were separated.
any more	I see my Dad sometimes,
	and he gives me a bit of money.
rooms in a private	But he is in lodgings,
house for which	and he's got a tumor
you pay money	on his brain.
grey cells in your	My Mum died in 1975,
head that make you	so I had to leave home.
think, feel, speak act	I had a baby, a little boy,
	called Mark,
	so I lived in an unmarried
	mothers' home in Wimbledon
	for a while.
tolerate (she didn't	But I couldn't stick that,
like it)	so I found a family
	to look after him
	and took a job,
	making lampshades.
	I stayed with a friend
some	for a couple of weeks,
allowed	but she was not supposed
people who live	to take lodgers,
in lodgings	and when they found out
thrown, kicked	I got chucked out.

Tasks

a) For better understanding write a short text about Janice showing most of her troubles and problems.

b) Write down a few suggestions as to what she could do perhaps to get settled and make a living.

c) Do you know anyone who has problems like Janice?

d) Compare Janice's problems and difficulties with those of Margaret in Calcutta. Make up two lists of notes.

Sandra Grant. The Sunday Telegraph.
Quoted from Alan Duff: That's Life.
Cambridge University Press 1979

4 The green years

(This story is set in South Africa. Lee is a young African who makes his living by doing various small jobs in houses and offices. Here he is talking to a Jewish girl in an office.)

"Lee."
I stopped and turned to her.
"That is your name, isn't it?"
"Yes, missus."
"Miss, not missus. You only say missus to a married woman."
Her smile encouraged me.
"We say it to all white women."
"Then you are wrong. Say miss."
"Yes, miss."
"That's better . . . Tell me, how old are you?"
"Going on for eleven, miss."
"Why don't you go to school?"
"I don't know, miss."
"Don't you want to?"
"I don't know, miss."
"Can you read or write?"
"No, miss."
"Stop saying miss now."
"Yes, miss."
She laughed.
"So you can't read?"
"No, miss."
"Wouldn't you like to?"
"I don't know, miss."
"Want to find out?"
"Yes, miss."
She turned the pages of the book in front of her. She looked at me, then began to read from Lambs Tales from Shakespeare. The story of Othello jumped at me and invaded my heart and mind as the young woman read. I was transported to the land where the brave Moor lived and loved and destroyed his love.
The young woman finished.
"Like it?"
"Oh yes!"
"Good. This book is full of stories like that. If you go to school you'll be able to read them for yourself."
"Here, I'm going to school."
"When?"
"Monday."
"I've started something." She laughed.
"But why didn't you go before?"
"Nobody told me."
"You must have seen other children go to school."
"Nobody told me about the stories."
"Oh yes, the stories."
"When I can read and write I'll make stories like that!"

(Peter Abrahams,
from MODERN AFRICAN PROSE)

Put it in writing

Shut your book and write a short summary.

First . . .
Then . . .
Finally . . .

What has this story to do with survival?

5 Can science help?

Ten thousand people are dying of hunger every day.

In poor countries one dollar could feed one person for at least a week.

Six hundred million dollars are being spent on arms every day.

What do these statistics mean?

If the rich countries gave enough help to the poor countries there would be enough food, shelter and medicine for everyone in the world.

What can be done?

There are many parts of the world that could grow more food with the technology and advances of the next decade. (See table below)

Skyscraper food

We can grow food in tall glass buildings. We don't need soil. We can feed the plants by using pipes which can take liquid food to them. The sun will provide heat for plants to grow all the year round, especially if the buildings are in the desert or on high ground.

The sea

Perhaps we will begin a new history when we begin to farm the sea, and live beneath it! The British Ministry of Agriculture and Fisheries says that we will grow fish like plants in fields.

A different opinion

Many people think that the main thing to do is *not* to grow more. There is enough for everyone now, they say. People are only starving because other people are greedy.

What do you think?

	hectares available	**What we must do**
LATIN AMERICA (BRAZIL)	450,000,000	Improve the soil and stop the rain washing it away.
PERU AND CHILE SEA COASTS	50,000,000	Use water from the sea to improve the land.
UNITED STATES OF AMERICA	100,000,000	Pay higher prices to American farmers so they will grow more and develop more land.
SAHARA DESERT, AFRICA	500–700,000,000	Bring water to the desert.

6 Survival summary

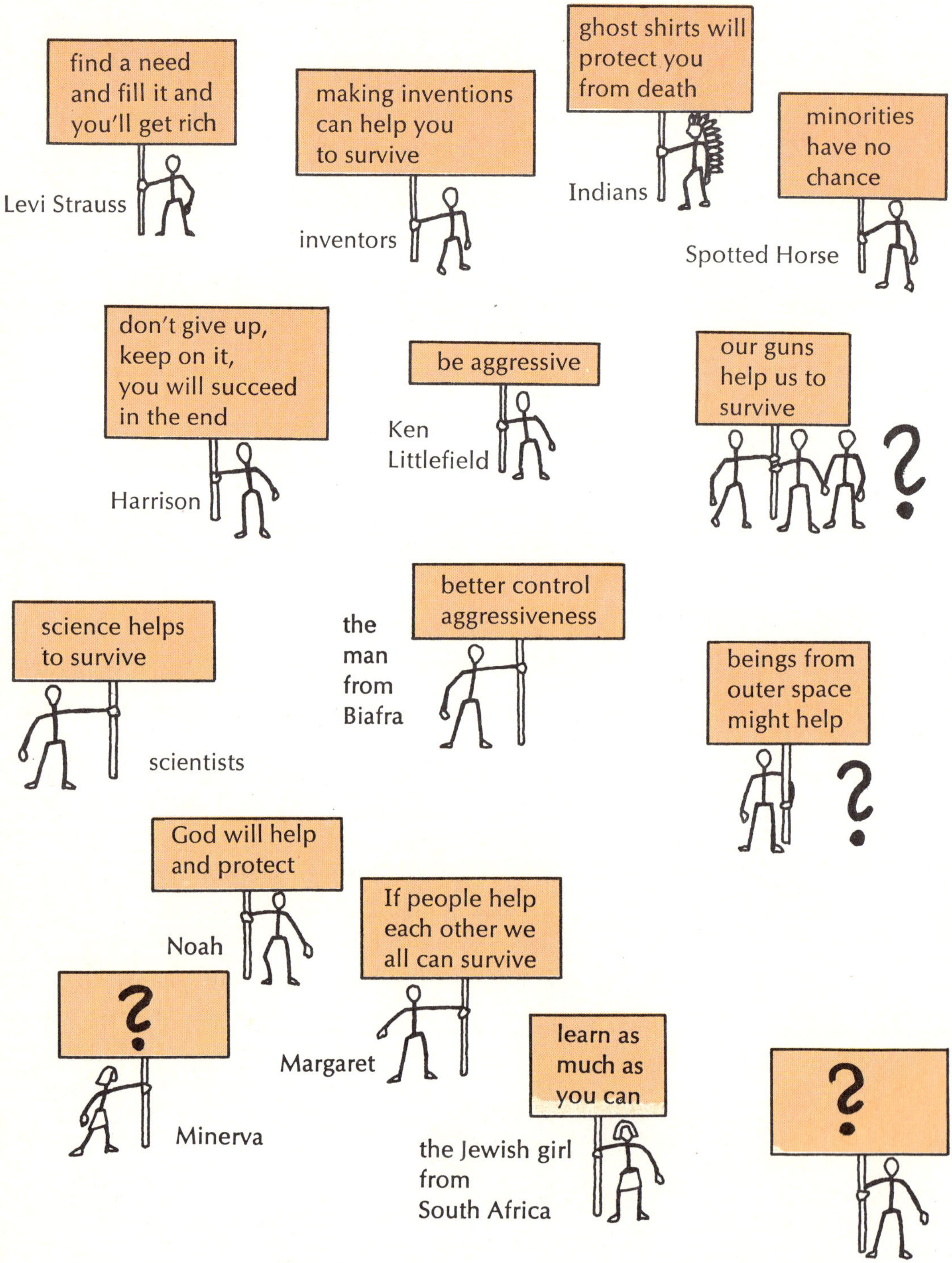

These drawings tell you what you have learned in other parts of this text book about survival. Draw a table like that one below and put the survival views in rank order. Add other possibilities you know.

	for the survival of the individual	for the survival of the human species
best chance		
next best chance		
...		
... only small chance		

Can we survive?

Look at the following statements about the future.
Decide which of them are optimistic and which are pessimistic.

Many people will die of hunger in India because there won't be enough food.

Man will solve the food problems in the world and no more people will die of starvation.

Computers will do all the work and man won't be needed.

Computers will do all the work and man will have more time for fun and relaxation.

Cities in the future will have many parks and green areas for people only.

People will stop driving cars and use more trains and buses to save energy.

The arctic zones will increase and cover the earth with ice.

Earthquakes and volcanoes will destroy thousands of people and communities in Asia.

People all over the world will stop fighting.

Tasks – **Classify:**

A – yes, very likely
B – possible
C – not very likely
D – impossible
E – no opinion

– Are you an optimist or pessimist about man's chances for survival? Write a paragraph describing your view.

Language aids I think, man might survive because . . .

7

Project 7

Focus on Germany

> "Life is too short to learn German."
>
> Thomas Love Peacock (1785–1866)
>
> Peacock was a writer. He wrote several novels with funny characters and witty dialogues.

Maybe you still have a few problems with English. Well, here you can read about the problems a famous American writer had with German!

The awful German language

In German, all the nouns begin with a capital letter. Now, that is a good idea in that language, because so you always know what is a noun the minute you see it. You make mistakes sometimes, because you take the name of a person for the name of a thing and waste much time, because you try to get a meaning out of it. German names almost always mean something, and this helps to confuse the student. I translated a passage one day which said that "the furious tiger ate up the poor Tannenwald as a whole." I was just going to doubt that, when I found out that Tannenwald was the name of a man. Another funny thing is the length of German words. Some of them are so long that they have a perspective. Take these examples:

FREUNDSCHAFTSBEZEIGUNGEN

STADTVERORDNETENVERSAMMLUNG

ALTERTUMSWISSENSCHAFTEN

WAFFENSTILLSTANDSVERHANDLUNGEN

These things are not words, they are alphabetical processions. And you can see them in every German newspaper marching majestically across the pages. I am very interested in these things. When I find a good one, I collect it and put in into my museum. I have already a very valuable collection.

Adapted from Mark Twain "A Tramp Abroad"

7

Project 7

Focus on other countries

Canada

Canada is over 3,8 million square miles in area. It is the second-largest country in the world, covering nearly half the North American continent. It has about 23,670,000 inhabitants. The capital is Ottawa.
You certainly think of these pictures, when you hear the name Canada:

Indian totem-poles

Canoeing on one of the lakes

The Canadian elk

Wild bears fishing in a river

But did you also know that

- 20 % of the population speak only French? That there is even a movement of people who want to be separate from the English speaking part of Canada?
- more than 750,000 sq.km of the country are covered with lakes, and that there are large areas which are totally uninhabited?
- nearly 300,000 Indians and 17,500 Eskimos live in Canada?

How do you become a Canadian citizen?

Canada's new immigration law, proclaimed on April 10, 1978, regulates how people may come into Canada: immigrants who come to stay for good, foreign students, temporary workers, tourists, business people and other visitors. There are 60 Canadian immigration offices in 40 countries around the world. Anyone wishing to immigrate must go to one of those offices.

There are three classes of immigrants:

- people who have relatives in Canada who sponsor them,
- refugees or asylants,
- people who want to live in Canada and are willing and able to become good Canadian citizens.

To qualify for citizenship an adult (18 years of age or older) must have lived and worked in Canada as a regular immigrant for at least three years. Applicants for citizenship must also be able to speak one of the official languages, English or French, have a knowledge of Canada and know his rights and responsibilities as a Canadian citizen. To become a Canadian citizen a person must

apply for citizenship
appear before a citizenship judge
for a hearing
and attend a ceremony to take the oath
of citizenship.

Task Can you explain how to become a German citizen?

7

Project 7

Language study package

MINI MODEL TEXTS

Survival. If I were alone in the wilderness I would need some tools to build a shelter and to trap animals. It would be nice to have a radio or some books or a pet there, too. I wouldn't need money. It is useless in the wilderness. For sick people medicine is important. Most of us need someone to talk to. And nobody can live without food and warmth and something to drink.

WORDS

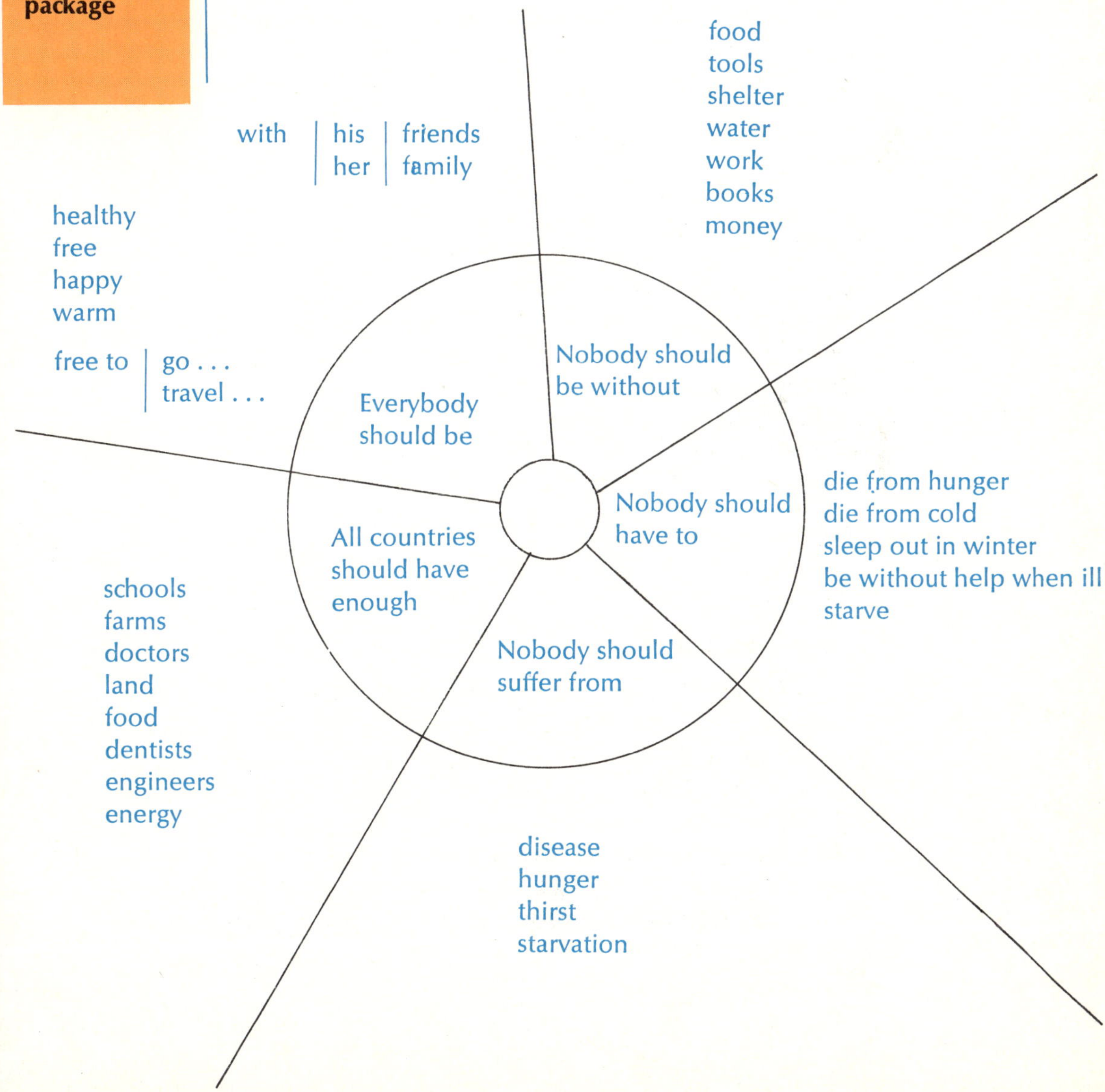

ACTIVE VOICE		
	indirect object	direct object
The teacher told	the pupils	a story.
The postman gave	Mother	a letter.
Janie offered	Mr. Jones	a cup of tea.

PASSIVE VOICE		
subject		direct object
The pupils	were told	a story.
Mother	was given	a letter.
Mr. Jones	was offered	a cup of tea.

Wenn ein Verb ein indirektes Objekt (eine oder mehrere Personen) und ein direktes Objekt (einen oder mehrere Gegenstände) hat, wird das indirekte Objekt normalerweise im Passivsatz zum Subjekt.

1. Put these sentences into the passive.

Noah built the ark before the big flood.
Kenneth Arnold saw a flying saucer in June 1947.
A member of the Waldgrave family kidnapped a French nun.
Henry Bull built Borley Rectory in 1863.
The ghost didn't disturb the puddles of water on the road.
A fox heard the quack frog talking.
Jupiter invited all the animals to the banquet.
Hercules kicked the apple with his foot.

2. Put the passive sentences into the active.

The snake was stung by a wasp several times.
The emergency service phone number can be called at any time.
Nearly half the North American continent is covered by Canada.
English or French must be spoken by people who want to become Canadians.
Father and son were photographed by reporters.
The 100 Centre Street boy was told by the judge to stand up straight.
"The Waltons" have been watched on TV by a lot of Americans and Germans.

Defining and non-defining relative clauses

Example a) Defining relative clauses

People who use more energy than necessary waste it.
(Which people? The people who use more energy . . .)

Here the relative clause is absolutely necessary.
Without it the meaning of the sentence is unclear.

Example b) Non-defining relative clauses

Pollution is dirt, which comes from factories, cars, and cities.

Here the relative clause is not necessary.
Without it, the meaning of the sentence is clear, too:
Pollution is dirt.

Defining relative clauses werden nicht durch Kommas vom Hauptsatz getrennt.

In defining relative clauses kann anstelle von WHO oder WHICH auch THAT benutzt werden.

Defining and non-defining relative clauses: practice

Fill in the blanks with the correct relative pronouns.
Which of the relative clauses is defining and which is non-defining?

Most Indians(,) . . . live in reservations don't find jobs.

The buffaloes(,) . . . were shot by the Sioux provided food and clothing.

The people(,) . . . travelled along the Oregon trail dreamed of a better life.

The guns(,) . . . were taken from the Indians at Wounded Knee were stacked in the center.

Penicillin is a medicine(,) . . . was invented by Sir A. Fleming.

The sweets(,) . . . are given to children at Halloween are wrapped in paper first.

The ghosts(,) . . . you see on Halloween are made from pumpkins.

The man(,) . . . invented dynamite was Alfred Nobel.

The clock(,) . . . was built by John Harrison was tested on a voyage to Jamaica.

William Spotted Horse is an Indian(,) . . . told us his biography.

Verb form revision: IRREGULAR VERBS

Simple form	Present participle	Past form	Past participle
be	being	was, were	been
become	becoming	became	become
begin	beginning	began	begun
bite	biting	bit	bitten
blow	blowing	blew	blown
break	breaking	broke	broken
bring	bringing	bought	brought
build	building	built	built
burn	burning	burned (burnt)	burned (burnt)
buy	buying	bought	bought
catch	catching	caught	caught
choose	choosing	chose	chosen
come	coming	came	come
cost	costing	cost	cost
cut	cutting	cut	cut
do	doing	did	done
draw	drawing	drew	drawn
dream	dreaming	dreamt	dreamt
drink	drinking	drank	drunk
drive	driving	drove	driven
eat	eating	ate	eaten
fall	falling	fell	fallen
feel	feeling	felt	felt
fight	fighting	fought	fought
find	finding	found	found
fly	flying	flew	flown
forget	forgetting	forgot	forgotten
get	getting	got	got
give	giving	gave	given
go	going	went	gone
grow	growing	grew	grown
hang	hanging	hung	hung
have	having	had	had
hear	hearing	heard	heard
hide	hiding	hid	hidden
hit	hitting	hit	hit
hold	holding	held	held
hurt	hurting	hurt	hurt
keep	keeping	kept	kept
know	knowing	knew	known
lead	leading	led	led
learn	learning	learned (learnt)	learned (learnt)
leave	leaving	left	left

Simple form	Present participle	Past form	Past participle
lend	lending	lent	lent
let	letting	let	let
lie	lying	lay	lain
lose	losing	lost	lost
make	making	made	made
mean	meaning	meant	meant
meet	meeting	met	met
put	putting	put	put
read	reading	read	read
rid	ridding	rid	rid
ride	riding	rode	ridden
run	running	ran	run
say	saying	said	said
see	sending	saw	seen
sell	seeing	sold	sold
send	sending	sent	sent
set	setting	set	set
shoot	shooting	shot	shot
show	showing	showed	showed (shown)
sing	singing	sang	sung
sit	sitting	sat	sat
sleep	sleeping	slept	slept
smell	smelling	smelled (smelt)	smelled (smelt)
speak	speaking	spoke	spoken
spend	spending	spent	spent
spread	spreading	spread	spread
stand	standing	stood	stood
steal	stealing	stole	stolen
stick	sticking	stuck	stuck
swim	swimming	swam	swum
take	taking	took	taken
teach	teaching	taught	taught
tear	tearing	tore	torn
tell	telling	told	told
think	thinking	thought	thought
throw	throwing	threw	thrown
try	trying	tried	tried
understand	understanding	understood	understood
wake	waking	woke	woken
wear	wearing	wore	worn
win	winning	won	won
write	writing	wrote	written

Vocabulary

	project	section	page
aboard	6	4	111
abolish	6	FO	116
absolute	7	S	120
acccent	6	2	106
accompany	5	FG	96
according to	3	4	56
accuracy	4	4	76
accurate	4	4	76
accuse	4	1	68
action	5	5	94
actual	2	3	32
adhesive	1	3	14
admiralty	4	4	74
admire	6	FO	117
advance (n)	7	5	129
advisable	4	FG	79
advise	2	1	29
aeroplane	4	S	66
afterwards	1	1	11
aggression	5	5	93
aggressiveness	5	5	86
aggressometer	5	1	88
aggressor	5	S	87
agriculture	7	5	129
aid (n)	3	3	51
aim (v)	3	4	54
airfare	5	FG	96
alphabetical	7	FG	132
alter	2	3	32
although	2	3	32
altitude	3	3	49
among	2	3	32
amulet	6	3	108
analyse	5	S	86
angel	5	S	87
anger (n)	5	3	90
apart	4	4	76
appear	6	2	107
applicant	7	FO	134
apply	7	FO	134
appreciate	5	FG	96
appropriate	3	FG	57
approximate	2	FO	36
arm	3	4	54
arrange	7	S	122
arrest (v)	3	4	53
arrogant	4	5	77
article	3	FO	57
aspect	6	FO	116
assistant	6	2	107
astronomy	4	4	73
asylant	7	FO	134
atlas	1	2	12
atmosphere	6	1	104
atomic	4	S	66
attack (v)	3	4	52

	project	section	page
attempt (v)	5	S	87
attend	7	FO	134
attention	5	3	90
attract	6	4	110
authentic	5	S	87
available	7	5	129
aware	5	4	91
awful	2	2	31
bagpipe	2	FO	35
balloon	4	S	66
bamboo	4	2	70
banknote	2	FO	36
banquet (n)	6	6	114
bare	5	LP	102
barrier	6	FO	116
base (v)	4	5	77
battle (n)	3	4	52
beam (n)	6	2	106
bear (v), bore, borne	2	2	31
bearded	5	S	87
beforehand	4	FG	79
behaviour	5	LP	100
believer	3	4	53
belong	2	FG	34
bend, bent, bent	2	1	29
beneath	7	5	129
bible	6	4	109
bicycle (n)	5	FG	96
bill (n)	3	FO	59
billion	4	FO	80
birth	4	5	77
blank	3	LP	62
blessing (n)	7	2	126
blood	4	5	94
bloody	3	4	52
blow, blew, blown	1	4	15
boarding school	3	S	45
bomb (n)	4	4	73
bonnet	4	FO	80
boot	4	FO	80
bore (n)	2	S	28
bother (v)	4	1	68
brain	7	3	127
brave (adj.)	7	4	128
brick up	6	5	112
brief (adj.)	5	FO	97
brochure	4	FG	79
broomstick	4	FO	81
bubble (n)	4	1	68
buffalo	3	S	42
bulb	4	2	70
bundle (n)	3	4	56
burst, burst, burst	6	2	106

	project	section	page
ca.	3	4	52
candle	1	S	7
canoeing (n)	7	FO	133
canvas	2	1	30
carbon	1	4	15
carbon dioxide	1	4	15
carbonize	4	2	70
cardboard	1	S	8
carnival	4	FG	80
carton	1	3	13
case (court)	5	4	91
caste	6	FO	116
cattleman	2	3	32
cause	3	5	54
celebrate	4	FO	81
cell	7	3	127
center (A. E.) (n)	3	4	55
centimeter	1	1	11
centre (n)	1	3	14
ceremony	3	3	48
chairman	4	FO	80
change (n)	4	4	76
chapter	5	S	87
characteristic (n)	7	1	125
charge (n)	4	FG	79
chase	5	LP	100
check (v)	6	1	104
chemistry	1	4	15
chief (n)	3	3	48
childbirth	7	2	126
childhood	4	2	70
china (n)	3	3	49
chip (n) (A. E.)	3	FO	80
christian	4	FO	81
chronometer	4	4	73
chuck	7	3	127
circle	1	3	13
citizenship	7	FO	134
civilian (n)	5	FO	98
claim (v)	6	2	106
classify	7	6	131
clause	5	LP	100
clean out (v)	4	FO	81
clerk	5	2	89
cliff	7	S	123
clip (n)	1	S	8
clockmaker	4	4	73
close (v)	1	1	10
closet (n)	4	FO	80
clothe, clad, clad	5	S	87
clothing	2	3	32
cloud (n)	1	S	7
club (n)	3	4	54
coarse	2	3	32
coast	7	5	129
cock (v)	5	3	90

S = Starters
FG = Focus on Germany
FO = Focus on other countries
LP = Language study package

Proper Names

Project 1 – Starters

experiment	ɪks'perɪmənt	Experiment
starter	'stɑ:tə	hier: zum Einstieg
candle	'kændl	Kerze
hollow	'hɒləʊ	hohl
waterproof	'wɔ:təpru:f	wasserdicht
miracle	'mɪrəkl	Wunder
weightlifter	'weɪtlɪftə	Gewichtheber
robot	'rəʊbɒt	Roboter
mask	mɑ:sk	Maske
cloud	klaʊd	Wolke
snowstorm	'snəʊstɔ:m	Schneesturm
test (v)	test	testen
fool (v)	fu:l	täuschen, hineinlegen
clip	klɪp	Klammer
pin	pɪn	Stecknadel
needle	'ni:dl	Nadel
a pair of scissors	ə peər‿əv 'sɪzəz	Schere
drawing pin	'drɔ:ɪŋ pɪn	Reißnagel
spool	spu:l	Spule
thread	θred	Faden
pen knife	'pen naɪf	Taschenmesser
screwdriver	'skru:draɪvə	Schraubenzieher
string	strɪŋ	Schnur
pincers	'pɪnsəz	Pinzette
flat pliers	flæt 'plaɪəz	Flachzange
paper fastener	'peɪpə 'fɑ:snə	Musterklammer
scotch tape	'skɒtʃ 'teɪp	Tesafilm
rubber band	'rʌbə bænd	Gummiring
cardboard	'kɑ:dbɔ:d	Pappe
punch	pʌntʃ	Locher
glue	glu:	Leim
form (v)	fɔ:m	bilden
central	'sentrəl	Haupt-
depot	'depəʊ	Lager, Sammelstelle
object	'ɒbdʒɪkt	Gegenstand
return (v)	rɪ'tɜ:n	zurückgeben
tool	tu:l	Werkzeug
teller	'telə	Stimmenzähler
jury	'dʒʊərɪ	(Preis)gericht
prize	praɪz	Preis

Project 1 – Experiment A

edge	edʒ	Rand
forefinger	'fɔ:fɪŋgə	Zeigefinger
zero	'zɪərəʊ	Null
touch	tʌtʃ	berühren
let go	let 'gəʊ	loslassen
close	kləʊz	schließen
mark (n)	mɑ:k	Markierung
thumb	θʌm	Daumen
rating	'reɪtɪŋ	Bewertung
centimeter	'sentɪmi:tə	Zentimeter
hundredth	'hʌndrədθ	Hundertstel
second	'sekənd	Sekunde
afterwards	'ɑ:ftəwədz	später
in the end	ɪn‿ðɪ‿'end	am Schluß

Project 1 – Experiment B

muscle	'mʌsl	Muskel
thick	θɪk	dick
dictionary	'dɪkʃənrɪ	Wörterbuch
atlas	'ætləs	Atlas
metre	'mi:tə	Meter
horizontal	hɒrɪ'zɒntl	waagerecht

Project 1 – Experiment C

gram	græm	Gramm
fit	fɪt	(an)passen
straw	strɔ:	Stroh(halm)
bottle top	'bɒtl tɒp	Verschlußkappe
toilet roll	'tɔɪlɪt rəʊl	Toilettenpapierrolle
tube	tju:b	Röhre
toothpaste	'tu:θpeɪst	Zahnpasta
carton	'kɑ:tən	Schachtel
flap	flæp	Klappe
shoulder	'ʃəʊldə	Schulter
pierce	'pɪəs	durchbohren
centre	'sentə	Mitte
operate	'ɒpəreɪt	hier: bedienen
adhesive	əd'hi:sɪv	haftend, klebend
detail	'di:teɪl	Einzelheit
unusual	ʌn'ju:ʒʊəl	ungewöhnlich
turn upside down	tɜ:n‿'ʌpsaɪd daʊn	auf den Kopf stellen
session	'seʃn	Sitzung
by the way	baɪ ðə 'weɪ	übrigens

Project 1 – Experiment D

torch	tɔ:tʃ	Taschenlampe
magnifying glass	'mægnɪfaɪɪŋ glɑ:s	Vergrößerungsglas
float	fləʊt	schweben
drop	drɒp	Tropfen
crystal	'krɪstl	Kristall
condense	kən'dens	kondensieren, verdichten
droplet	'drɒplɪt	Tröpfchen
mixture	'mɪkstʃə	Mischung
mash	mæʃ	(zer)stampfen
blow, blew, blown	bləʊ, blu:, bləʊn	blasen
direct	'daɪrekt	direkt
shine, shone, shone	ʃaɪn, ʃɒn, ʃɒn	scheinen
chemistry	'kemɪstrɪ	Chemie
physics	'fɪzɪks	Physik
solid	'sɒlɪd	fest
carbon dioxide	'kɑ:bən daɪ'ɒksaɪd	Kohlendioxyd
watch out	wɒtʃ‿aʊt	aufpassen
discourse	dɪs'kɔ:s	Unterhaltung
glue (v)	glu:	aufkleben
slip off	slɪp‿ɒf	abrutschen

Project 1 – Experiment E

screw (n)	skru:	Schraube
jar	dʒɑ:	Einmachglas
millimetre	'mɪlɪmi:tə	Millimeter
stick out	stɪk‿'aut	überstehen, vorstehen
light, lighted/lit	laɪ, 'laɪtɪd/lɪt	anzünden
wax	wæks	Wachs

Project 1 – Experiment F

nylon	'naɪlən	Nylon
stocking	'stɒkɪŋ	Strumpf
gauze	gɔ:z	Gaze
elastic band	ɪ'læstɪk bænd	Gummiband
fasten	'fɑ:sn	befestigen
tap	tæp	Wasserhahn
fabric	'fæbrɪk	Stoff
full	fʊl	voll

Project 1 – Experiment G

place (v)	pleɪs	setzen, stellen, legen
wet (v)	wet	befeuchten
as well	əz 'wel	auch
result	rɪ'zʌlt	Ergebnis

Project 1 – Focus on Germany

focus	'fəʊkəs	Brennpunkt
prepare	prɪ'peə	vorbereiten
foreigner	'fɒrənə	Ausländer
explain	ɪks'pleɪn	erklären
guidebook	'gaɪdbʊk	Reiseführer
bus stop	bʌs stɒp	Bushaltestelle
suburb	'sʌbɜ:b	Vorort
initial	ɪ'nɪʃəl	Anfangs-buchstabe
youth centre	ju:θ 'sentə	Jugendzentrum
particular	pə'tɪkjʊlə	besonders
explanation	ekspIə'neɪʃən	Erklärung
postal rate	'pəʊstəl reɪt	Portogebühr
telephone code	'telɪfəʊn kəʊd	Verzeichnis der Vorwahlnummern
telephone call	'telɪfəʊn kɔ:l	Telefongespräch
means	mi:nz	Mittel
transportation	trænspɔ:'teɪʃn	Verkehr
costs (n)	kɒsts	Kosten
folder	'fəʊldə	Schnellhefter

Project 1 – Focus on other countries

souvenir	'su:vənɪə	Reiseandenken
sign	saɪn	Zeichen
native language	'neɪtɪv 'læŋgwɪdʒ	Muttersprache
population	pɒpjʊ'leɪʃn	Bevölkerung
Hindi	'hɪndi:	Hindi
Russian	'rʌʃən	russisch
Arabic	'ærəbɪk	arabisch
Bengali	beŋ'gɔ:lɪ	bengalisch
Portuguese	pɔ:tjʊ'gi:z	portugiesisch
Japanese	dʒæpə'ni:z	japanisch
Malay	mə'leɪ	malaiisch
colony	'kɒlənɪ	Kolonie
formerly	'fɔ:məlɪ	früher, ehemals
Gaelic	'geɪlɪk	gälisch
Irish	'aɪrɪʃ	irisch
official	ə'fɪʃəl	offiziell, Amts-

Project 2 – Starters

motorbiking	'məʊtəbaɪkɪŋ	Motorradfahren
tiger	'taɪgə	Tiger
king	kɪŋ	König
'cept (= except)	sept, ɪk'sept	außer
wake up, woke up, woken up	weɪk‿ʌp, wəʊk‿ʌp, 'wəʊkən‿ʌp	aufwachen
commercial	kə'mɜ:ʃl	hier: Reklame
denim	'denɪm	Stoffart
dungaree	dʌŋgə'ri:	Stoffart
indigo	'ɪndɪgəʊ	indigoblau
Indian	'ɪndjən	indisch
heel	hi:l	Ferse, Absatz
all day long	ɔ:l deɪ lɒŋ	den ganzen Tag
sloppy	'slɒpɪ	schlampig
just	dʒʌst	einfach, nur
romp	rɒmp	(herum)toben
pup	pʌp	Welpe
shirt-tail	'ʃɜ:t teɪl	Hemdzipfel
step out	step‿aʊt	heraustreten
shore	ʃɔ:	Strand, Ufer
marvellous	'mɑ:vələs	wunderbar
suppose	sə'pəʊz	annehmen, vermuten
bore (n)	bɔ:	Langweiler
pose	pəʊz	sich in Positur stellen
dressed-up clothes	drest‿ʌp kləʊðz	feine Kleider
pretend	prɪ'tend	vorgeben, so tun als ob
Genoa	dʒe'nəʊə	Genua
gold digger	'gəʊld 'dɪgə	Goldgräber
high	haɪ	hier: gut gelaunt, hochgestimmt
tight	taɪt	eng

Project 2 – The Jeans Stories

1.

Norwegian	nɔ:'wi:dʒən	norwegisch
Gold Rush	'gəʊld rʌʃ	Goldrausch
Bavaria	bə'veərɪə	Bayern
Serge	sɜ:dʒ	Serge (Name einer Stoffart)
cover	'kʌvə	Bedeckung, Plane
pants	pænts	Hosen
wear out, wore out, worn out	weər‿aʊt, wɔ:r‿aʊt, wɔ:n‿aʊt	abtragen

advise	əd'vaɪz	beraten
tailor	'teɪlə	Schneider
have someone make	hæv 'sʌmwʌn meɪk	jemanden herstellen lassen
please (v)	pli:z	zufriedenstellen
manufacture	mænjʊ'fæktʃə	herstellen
ride, rode, ridden	raɪd, rəʊd, 'rɪdn	reiten
low cut	ləʊ kʌt	tief angeschnitten
bend, bent, bent	bend, bent, bent	beugen, bücken
complain	kəm'pleɪn	(sich) beklagen
keep, kept, kept	ki:p, kept, kept	hier: etwas immer wieder tun
metal	'metl	Metall
get fitted up	get 'fɪtɪd‿ʌp	ausgestattet werden
canvas	'kænvəs	Leinwand
profit	'prɒfɪt	Gewinn
laugh	lɑ:f	lachen

2.

success	sək'ses	Erfolg
formula	'fɔ:mjʊlə	Formel
bear, bore, borne	beə, bɔ:, bɔ:n	ertragen, aushalten
hard wear	hɑ:d 'weə	Strapaze
tear (n)	'teə	Riß
propaganda	prɒpə'gændə	Werbung
practical	'præktɪkl	praktisch
awful	'ɔ:ful	scheußlich
pink	pɪŋk	rosa
make (n)	meɪk	Machart

3.

cattleman	'kætlmæn	Cowboy
common	'kɒmən	hier: üblich, verbreitet
although	ɔ:l'ðəʊ	obwohl
connection	kə'nekʃən	Verbindung
garment	'gɑ:mənt	Kleidungsstück
actually	'æktʃʊəlɪ	tatsächlich
alter	'ɔ:ltə	ändern
weave, wove, woven	wi:v, wəʊv, 'wəʊvn	weben
similar	'sɪmɪlə	ähnlich
phrase	freɪz	Ausdruck
exotic	ɪg'zɒtɪk	exotisch
fabled	'feɪbld	märchenhaft
coarse	kɔ:s	grob
clothing	'kləʊðɪŋ	Bekleidung
merchant	'mɜ:tʃənt	Händler, Kaufmann
method	'meθəd	Methode, Verfahren
shut, shut, shut	ʃʌt, ʃʌt, ʃʌt,	schließen
short	ʃɔ:t	kurz
paragraph	'pærəgrɑ:f	Abschnitt

4.

false	fɔ:ls	falsch
rivet	'rɪvɪt	Niete
ore	ɔ:	Erz
standard	'stændəd	Standard
load	ləʊd	(be)laden
emigrant	'emɪgrənt	Auswanderer

Project 2 – Focus on Germany

view (n)	vju:	Aussicht
live on	lɪv‿ɒn	von etwas leben
liver	'lɪvə	Leber
soft drink	sɒft drɪŋk	alkoholfreies Getränk
reasonable	'ri:znəbl	vernünftig
delicacy	'delɪkəsɪ	Delikatesse
sort	sɔ:t	Sorte, Art
Greek	gri:k	griechisch
Balkan	'bɔ:lkən	balkanesisch
Vietnamese	vjetnə'mi:z	vietnamesisch
delicious	dɪ'lɪʃəs	köstlich

Project 2 – Focus on other countries

United Kingdom	ju:'naɪtɪd 'kɪŋdəm	Vereinigtes Königreich (von Großbritannien)
consist of	kən'sɪst‿ɒv	bestehen aus
size	saɪz	Größe
sq. km. (square kilometre)	skweə 'kɪləʊmɪtə	Quadrat-kilometer
approximate	ə'prɒksɪmət	annähernd, ungefähr
have in mind	hæv‿ɪn maɪnd	an etwas denken
kilt	kɪlt	Kilt, Schottenrock
bagpipe	'bægpaɪp	Dudelsack
loch	lɒx	schottisch: See
graze	greɪz	weiden
violent	'vaɪələnt	heftig, gewaltsam
defeat	dɪ'fi:t	besiegen
century	'sentʃʊrɪ	Jahrhundert
industrial	ɪn'dʌstrɪəl	industriell
revolution	revə'lu:ʃən	Revolution
mining	'maɪnɪŋ	Bergbau
production	prə'dʌkʃən	Erzeugung
steel	sti:l	Stahl
develop	dɪ'veləp	entwickeln
especial	e'speʃl	besonders
Scot	skɒt	Schotte
banknote	'bæŋknəʊt	Banknote
independent	ɪndɪ'pendənt	unabhängig
import	'ɪmpɔ:t	Einfuhr

Project 3 – Starters

Indian	'ɪndjən	Indianer
hunt	hʌnt	jagen
buffalo	'bʌfələʊ	Büffel
Apache	ə'pætʃɪ	Apache
express (n)	ɪks'pres	Expreß, Eilbeförderung
squaw	skwɔ:	Indianerfrau
battle	'bætl	Schlacht
tomahawk	'tɒməhɔ:k	Kriegsbeil
uranium	jʊ'reɪnjəm	Uran
prairie	'preərɪ	Steppe
Comanche	kə'mæntʃɪ	Komanche
dance (n)	dɑ:ns	Tanz
peace	pi:s	Frieden
Pilgrim Fathers	'pɪlgrɪm 'fɑ:ðəz	Pilgerväter

torture (n)	'tɔ:tʃə	Marter
pole	pəʊl	Pfahl
nuclear power	'nju:klɪə 'paʊə	Atomkraft
sacred	'seɪkrɪd	heilig
pit	pɪt	Grube, Bergwerk
reservation	rezə'veɪʃn	Reservation
tribe	traɪb	Stamm
kid	kɪd	Kind
boarding school	'bɔ:dɪŋ sku:l	Internatsschule
not . . . at all	nɒt ət‿ɔ:l	überhaupt nicht
drop out	drɒp‿aʊt	vorzeitig abgehen
depressing	dɪ'presɪŋ	bedrückend
living conditions	'lɪvɪŋ kən'dɪʃnz	Lebensbedingungen
drug	drʌg	Droge
commit suicide	kə'mɪt 'sjʊɪsaɪd	Selbstmord begehen
trained	treɪnd	ausgebildet
prepare	prɪ'peə	vorbereiten
might	maɪt	könnte

Project 3 – The Old West

1.

northern	'nɔ:ðən	nördlich
seed	si:d	Same
gatherer	'gæðərə	Sammler
pueblo	pu'ebləʊ	Pueblo (indianische Hausform)
desert (n)	'dezət	Wüste
dweller	'dwelə	Siedler
topographical	tɒpə'græfɪkl	topographisch
locate	ləʊ'keɪt	orten, ausfindig machen
woodsman	'wʊdsmən	Waldbewohner
eastern	'i:stən	östlich
forest	'fɒrɪst	Wald
general	'dʒenərəl	allgemein
geographical	dʒɪə'græfɪkl	geographisch
location	ləʊ'keɪʃn	Ort, Lage
feature	'fi:tʃə	Zug
range	reɪndʒ	Kette
present (adj)	'preznt	gegenwärtig, heutig

2.

continent	'kɒntɪnənt	Erdteil
cross (v)	krɒs	überqueren
Bering Strait	'berɪŋ 'streɪt	Bering Straße
spread	spred	sich verbreiten
throughout	θru'aʊt	überall in
just as	'dʒʌst‿əz	ebenso wie
anyway	'enɪweɪ	sowieso,
factor	'fæktə	hier: Einfluß
Spanish	'spænɪʃ	spanisch
midwestern	'mɪd'westən	mittelwestlich
on horseback	ɒn 'hɔ:sbæk	zu Pferde
band	bænd	Bande, Gruppe
permanent	'pɜ:mənənt	ständig, Dauer-
nomad	'nəʊmæd	Nomade
herd	hɜ:d	Herde
tepee	'ti:pi:	Tipi (Indianerzelt)
blanket	'blæŋkɪt	Decke
horn	hɔ:n	Horn
hoof	hu:f	Huf
weapon	'wepən	Waffe
because of	bɪkɒz‿əv	wegen
shelter	'ʃeltə	Schutz, Behausung
chief	tʃi:f	Häuptling
courage	'kʌrɪdʒ	Mut
order	'ɔ:də	Befehl
religious	rɪ'lɪdʒəs	religiös
ceremony	'serɪmənɪ	Zeremonie
in return for	ɪn rɪ'tɜ:n fɔ:	als Gegengabe für

3.

trail	treɪl	Pfad, Fährte
overland	'əʊvəlænd	Überland –, auf dem Landweg
present day	'preznt 'deɪ	heutig
distance	'dɪstəns	Entfernung
altitude	'æltɪtju:d	Höhe
experience (v)	ɪks'pɪərɪəns	erfahren
china	'tʃaɪnə	Porzellan
goods	gʊdz	Waren
destination	destɪ'neɪʃn	Bestimmung(sort)
Presbyterian	prezbɪ'tɪərɪən	Presbyterianer
minister	'mɪnɪstə	Geistlicher
well-educated	'wel‿'edjʊkeɪtɪd	gebildet
successful	sək'sesfʊl	erfolgreich
wilderness	'wɪldənɪs	Wildnis
trek	trek	Treck
neighbour	'neɪbə	Nachbar
hot-tempered	hɒt 'tempəd	hitzig, aufbrausend
fist	fɪst	Faust
fight (n)	faɪt	Kampf
secure	sɪ'kjʊə	sicher
wagon master	'wægən 'mɑ:stə	Anführer des Trecks
pilot	'paɪlət	Führer
route	ru:t	Marschroute
resting place	'restɪŋ pleɪs	Rastplatz
scout	skaʊt	Fährtensucher
aid	eɪd	Hilfe

4.

timeline	'taɪm'laɪn	Zeittafel
ca.	'sɜ:kə	ungefähr, circa
seminomadic	semɪnəʊ'mædɪk	halbnomadisch
northward	'nɔ:θwəd	in nördlicher Richtung
migrate	maɪ'greɪt	wandern
westward	'westwəd	in westlicher Richtung
settler	'setlə	Siedler
attack (v)	ə'tæk	angreifen
invader	ɪn'veɪdə	Eindringling
fort	fɔ:t	Fort, befestigtes Vorwerk
wage war	weɪdʒ 'wɔ:	Krieg führen
bloody	'blʌdɪ	blutig
treaty	'tri:tɪ	Vertrag
include	ɪn'klu:d	einschließen
immediate	ɪ'mi:djət	sofort
settle	'setl	sich ansiedeln
defend	dɪfend	verteidigen

total	'təʊtl	völlig, vollständig
one by one	'wʌn baɪ 'wʌn	einer nach dem anderen
defeat	dɪ'fi:t	besiegen
cut in half	'kʌt‿ɪn 'hɑ:f	halbieren
divide	dɪ'vaɪd	teilen
seperate (adj)	'seprət	getrennt
starve	stɑ:v	verhungern
measles	'mi:zlz	Masern
epidemic	epɪ'demɪk	Epidemie, Seuche
desperation	despə'reɪʃən	Verzweiflung
plan (v)	plæn	planen
revolt	rɪ'vəʊlt	Aufstand
support	sə'pɔ:t	unterstützen
dance	dɑ:ns	Tanz
believer	bɪ'li:və	Glaubender
disappear	dɪsə'pɪə	verschwinden
outlaw (v)	'aʊtlɔ:	verbieten
arrest	ə'rest	festnehmen
teach, taught, taught	ti:tʃ, tɔ:t, tɔ:t	lehren
order (v)	'ɔ:də	befehlen, anordnen
submit	səb'mɪt	unterwerfen
desperate	'despərət	verzweifelt

5.

number (v)	'nʌmbə	zählen
surrender	sə'rendə	sich ergeben
creek	kri:k	Flüßchen
produce	prə'dju:s	hier: hervorheben
search (v)	sɜ:tʃ	durchsuchen
hide, hid, hidden	haɪd, hɪd, 'hɪdn	verstecken
search (n)	sɜ:tʃ	Durchsuchung
all of a sudden	ɔ:l‿əv‿ə 'sʌdn	plötzlich
fire (v)	'faɪə	feuern, schießen
troops	tru:ps	Truppen
shot	ʃɒt	Schuß
aim (v)	eɪm	zielen
confusion	kən'fju:ʒn	Verwirrung
ravine	rə'vi:n	Hohlweg
wherever	weər'evə	wo (auch) immer
pursue	pə'sju:	verfolgen
redskin	'redskɪn	Rothaut
escape	ɪ'skeɪp	entkommen
hero (pl. heroes)	'hɪərəʊ (hɪərəʊz)	Held
deed	di:d	Tat
daring	'deərɪŋ	Kühnheit
arm (v)	ɑ:m	bewaffnen
club	klʌb	Knüppel
conference	'kɔnfərəns	Konferenz
end (v)	end	enden, aufhören
demand	dɪ'mɑ:nd	verlangen
flee, fled, fled	fli:, fled, fled	fliehen
wound (v)	wu:nd	verwunden
hiding place	'haɪdɪŋ pleɪs	Versteck
sight	saɪt	Sicht
version	'vɜ:ʃən	Version, Fassung
arms (n)	ɑ:m	Waffe
stack up	stæk ʌp	stapeln
center	'sentə	Mitte
bundle	'bʌndl	Bündel
stake	steɪk	Stange
pile	paɪl	anhäufen
according to	ə'kɔ:dɪŋ tu:	gemäß, nach, laut
document	'dɒkjument	Dokument
willing	'wɪlɪŋ	bereitwillig

on purpose	ɒn 'pɜ:pəs	mit Absicht
by accident	baɪ‿'æksɪdənt	aus Versehen
illustrate	'ɪləstreɪt	illustrieren

Project 3 – Focus on Germany

public	'pʌblɪk	öffentlich
observe	əb'zɜ:v	beachten
New Year's Day	'nju: jɜ:z deɪ	Neujahrstag
Good Friday	gʊd 'fraɪdɪ	Karfreitag
Easter	'i:stə	Ostern
Labour Day	'leɪbə deɪ	Tag der Arbeit
Ascension Day	ə'senʃn deɪ	Himmelfahrt
Whit Monday	wɪt 'mʌndɪ	Pfingstmontag
Christmas Eve	'krɪsməs i:v	Heiliger Abend
Boxing Day	'bɔksɪŋ deɪ	2. Weihnachtstag
New Year's Eve	'nju: jɜ:z‿i:v	Sylvester
origin	'ɒrɪdʒɪn	Ursprung
Epiphany	ɪ'pɪfənɪ	Dreikönigstag
Rose Monday	rəʊz 'mʌndɪ	Rosenmontag
Shrove Tuesday	ʃrəʊv 'tju:zdɪ	Fastnachtsdienstag
peak	pi:k	Gipfel, Höhepunkt
carnival	'kɑ:nɪvəl	Karneval
appropriate	ə'prəʊprɪɪt	passend, jeweilig
Corpus Christi	'kɔ:pəs 'krɪstɪ	Fronleichnam
Whitsun	'wɪtsn	Pfingsten
Assumption Day	'əsʌmpʃn deɪ	Mariä Himmelfahrt
All Saints Day	ɔ:l 'seɪnts deɪ	Allerheiligen
Day of Prayer and Repentence	deɪ‿əv preə ənd rɪ'pentəns	Buß- und Bettag
supermarket	'su:pəmɑ:kɪt	Supermarkt
discount	'dɪskaʊnt	Diskont
leather	'leðə	Leder
mug	mʌg	Krug
junk	dʒʌŋk	Trödel, Schund

Project 3 – Focus on other countries

federal	'fedərəl	Bundes-
parliamentary	pɑ:lə'mentərɪ	parlamentarisch
Dutch	dʌtʃ	holländisch
including	ɪn'klu:dɪŋ	einschließlich
Aboriginal	æbə'rɪdʒənl	Ureinwohner
gather	'gæðə	Sammeln
root	ru:t	Wurzel
wise	waɪz	weise
holy	'həʊlɪ	heilig
fossil	'fɒsl	urzeitliche Versteinerung
strange	streɪndʒ	sonderbar, fremdartig
fauna	'fɔ:nə	Tierwelt
species	'spi:ʃi:z	Art
spiny anteater	'spaɪnɪ‿'ænti:tə	Ameisenigel
spine	spaɪn	Stachel
rather	'rɑ:ðə	hier: beinahe
hedgehog	'hedʒhɒg	Igel
insect	'ɪnsekt	Insekt
pest	pest	Schädling
koala bear (n)	kəʊ'ɑ:lə beə	Koalabär
leaf (pl leaves)	li:f (li:vz)	Blatt (vom Baum)
eucalyptus	ju:kə'lɪptəs	Eukalyptus

platypus	'plætɪpəs	Schnabeltier
furry	'fɜ:rɪ	pelzig
bill	bɪl	Schnabel
poisonous	'pɒɪznəs	giftig
spike	spaɪk	Stachel

Project 4 – Starters

diesel	'di:zəl	Diesel
engine	'endʒɪn	Maschine
radium	'reɪdjəm	Radium
gramophone	'græməfəʊn	Grammophon
lightning conductor	'laɪtnɪŋ kən'dʌktə	Blitzableiter
penicillin	penɪ'sɪlɪn	Penizillin
pendulum	'pendjʊləm	Pendel
postage	'pəʊstɪdʒ	Post-, Brief-
print	prɪnt	drucken
wireless telegraphy	'waɪələs tɪ'legrəfɪ	drahtlose Telegraphie
steam	sti:m	Dampf
turbine	'tɜ:bɪn	Turbine
atomic	ə'tɒmɪk	atomar, Atom-
structure	'strʌktʃə	Struktur, Aufbau
balloon	bə'lu:n	Ballon
photography	fə'tɒgrəfɪ	Fotographie
typewriter	'taɪpraɪtə	Schreibmaschine
locomotive	'ləʊkə'məʊtɪv	Lokomotive
aeroplane	'eərəpleɪn	Flugzeug
rank (v)	ræŋk	ordnen, aufzählen
scale	skeɪl	Skala
bucket	'bʌkɪt	Eimer
illness	'ɪlnəs	Krankheit
survival	sə'vaɪvəl	Überleben

Project 4 – Inventions

1.

bubble	'bʌbl	(Seifen-)blase
diagram	'daɪəgræm	Plan, Schema
for godssake	fə 'gɒdsseɪk	um Gotteswillen
bother	'bɒðə	stören
grandma	'grænmɑ:	Oma
underwear	'ʌndəweə	Unterwäsche
accuse	ə'kju:z	anklagen
finger	'fɪŋgə	Finger
soapy	'səʊpɪ	seifig, Seifen-
compartment	kəm'pɑ:tmənt	Kammer
trigger-actuated	'trɪgər‿'æktjʊeɪtɪd	durch einen Hebel in Tätigkeit gesetzt
pump	pʌmp	Pumpe
hose	həʊz	Schlauch
ring (n)	rɪŋ	Ring
fill-up	fɪl‿ʌp	Auffüll-
plug	plʌg	Stöpsel
air	'eə	Luft
compressor	kəm'presə	Kompressor, Verdichter
nozzle	'nɒzl	Mundstück, Ventil
operation	ɒpə'reɪʃn	hier: Bedienung
compress	kəm'pres	zusammenpressen
trigger	'trɪgə	Auslöser, Abzug
draw, drew, drawn	drɔ:, dru:, drɔ:n	ziehen
release	rɪ'li:z	befreien, freigeben
library	'laɪbrərɪ	Bücherei

2.

tie (v)	taɪ	binden
generate	'dʒenəreɪt	erzeugen
stroke	strəʊk	streichen
carbon	'kɑ:bən	Kohlenstoff
disc	dɪsk	Scheibe
sound (n)	saʊnd	Klang
transmit	trəns'mɪt	übertragen
phonograph	'fəʊnəgrɑ:f	Phonograph (Vorläufer des Plattenspielers)
machine	mə'ʃi:n	Gerät, Apparat
childhood	'tʃaɪldhʊd	Kindheit
carbonize	'kɑ:bənaɪz	verkohlen
bamboo	bæm'bu:	Bambus
that did the trick	ðæt dɪd ðə trɪk	damit gelang es
commercial	kə'mɜ:ʃəl	verkäuflich
bulb	bʌlb	Glühbirne
glow	gləʊ	glühen
improve	ɪm'pru:v	verbessern

3.

inventor	ɪn'ventə	Erfinder
use (n)	ju:s	Gebrauch
brick	brɪk	Ziegelstein
generator	'dʒenəreɪtə	Generator
match (n)	mætʃ	Streichholz
point	pɔɪnt	Spitze
face (v)	feɪs	gerichtet sein
everyday	'evrɪdeɪ	alltäglich
genius	'dʒɪ:njəs	Genie
even	'i:vən	gerade
fold	fəʊld	falten
procedure	prə'si:dʒə	Vorgehen, Verfahren
consideration	kənsɪdə'reɪʃen	Erwägung
I'm afraid	aɪm‿ə'freɪd	ich fürchte

4.

what's it all about?	wɒts ɪt ɔ:l ə'baʊt	worum geht es?
chronometer	krə'nɒmɪtə	Zeitmesser, Schiffsuhr
spacecraft	'speɪskrɑ:ft	Raumfahrzeug
physics	'fɪzɪks	Physik
astronomy	əs'trɒnəmɪ	Astronomie, Himmelskunde
longitude	'lɒndʒɪtju:d	geographische Länge
thermometer	θə'mɒmɪtə	Thermometer
bomb (n)	bɒm	Bombe
position	pə'zɪʃn	Position, Standort
navigation	nævɪ'geɪʃən	Navigation
clockmaker	'klɒkmeɪkə	Uhrmacher
marine	mə'ri:n	Marine
travel	'trævl	reisen
navigator	'nævɪgeɪtə	Navigator, Schiffsführer
determine	dɪ'tɜ:mɪn	bestimmen

error	'erə	hier: Abweichung
off course	ɒf 'kɔ:s	vom Kurs abgewichen
flagship	'flægʃɪp	Flaggschiff
wreck (v)	rek	scheitern
Admiralty	'ædmərəltɪ	Admiralität
set up	set‿ʌp	bilden, einsetzen
board	bɔ:d	hier: Amt, Ausschuß
enter	'entə	hier: einreichen
reduce	rɪ'dju:s	verringern
size	saɪz	Umfang, Maß
supervision	su:pə'vɪʒn	Überwachung
voyage	'vɒɪɪdʒ	Seereise
range	reɪndʒ	reichen
tropical	'trɒpɪkəl	tropisch
polar	'pəʊlə	polar
refuse	rɪ'fju:z	(sich) weigern
appeal to	ə'pi:l tʊ	sich wenden an
king	kɪŋ	König
right	raɪt	in Ordnung bringen
age	eɪdʒ	Alter
detective	dɪ'tektɪv	Detektiv
existence	ɪg'zɪstəns	Dasein
apart	ə'pɑ:t	auseinander
mechanism	'mekənɪzəm	Mechanismus
various	'veərɪəs	verschieden
change (n)	tʃeɪndʒ	Änderung
increase	ɪn'kri:s	vergrößern
accuracy	'ækjʊrəsɪ	Genauigkeit
accurate	'ækjʊrɪt	genau
rough	rʌf	rauh
reliable	rɪ'laɪəbl	zuverlässig
improvement	ɪm'pru:vmənt	Verbesserung
performance	pə'fɔ:məns	Leistung
direct (adj)	dɪ'rekt	direkt, geradewegs
Royal Observatory	'rɔɪəl‿əb'zɜ:vətrɪ	Königliches Observatorium
maybe	'meɪbi:	vielleicht

5.

birth	bɜ:θ	Geburt
conflict	'kɒnflɪkt	Konflikt, Streitfall
patient	'peɪʃnt	geduldig
dishonest	dɪs'ɒnɪst	unehrlich
arrogant	'ærəʊgənt	überheblich
creative	kri:'eɪtɪv	schöpferisch
trustworthy	'trʌstwɜ:ðɪ	vertrauenswürdig, zuverlässig
watch	wɒtʃ	Armbanduhr
run slow	rʌn sləʊ	nachgehen (Uhr)
rely on	rɪ'laɪ‿ɒn	sich verlassen auf
overwind, overwound, overwound	əʊvə'waɪnd, əʊvə'waʊnd, əʊvə'waʊnd	überdrehen
a.m. (ante meridiem)	'eɪ 'em 'æntɪ mə'rɪdɪəm	vor Mittag
p.m. (post meridiem)	'pi: 'em pəʊst mə'rɪdɪem	nach Mittag
take place	teɪk pleɪs	stattfinden
distinguish	dɪ'stɪŋgwɪʃ	unterscheiden
zone	zəʊn	Zone, Gebietsstreifen
necessity	nɪ'sesətɪ	Notwendigkeit
opposite	'ɒpəzɪt	gegenüber
proverb	'prɒvɜ:b	Sprichwort

Project 4 – Focus on Germany

keep in touch	ki:p‿ɪn 'tʌtʃ	in Verbindung bleiben
communicate	kə'mju:nɪkeɪt	in Verbindung treten
the latest	ðe 'leɪtɪst	das Neueste
date	deɪt	hier: Verabredung
call box	'kɔ:l bɒks	Telefonzelle
advisable	əd'vaɪzəbl	ratsam
enquiry	ɪn'kwaɪərɪ	Erkundigung
beforehand	bɪ'fɔ:hænd	zuvor
charge (n)	tʃɑ:dʒ	Gebühr
in addition to	ɪn‿ə'dɪʃn tə	zusätzlich zu
recognize	'rekəgnaɪz	erkennen
payphone	'peɪfəʊn	Münzfernsprecher
depict	dɪ'pɪkt	abbilden
STD (Subscriber trunk dialling)	es ti: di: səb'skraɪbə trʌŋk 'daɪəlɪŋ	Selbstwählferndienst
telegram	'telɪgræm	Telegramm
sheet	ʃi:t	Blatt
leaflet	'li:flɪt	Merkblatt
brochure	'brəʊʃə	Prospekt
unfortunately	ʌn'fɔ:tʃnətlɪ	leider, unglücklicherweise
counter	'kaʊntə	Schalter, Ladentheke
telephone directory	'telɪfəʊn dɪ'rektərɪ	Telefonbuch

Project 4 – Focus on other countries

correspondent	kɒrɪs'pɒndənt	Entsprechung
autumn **fall**	'ɔ:təm fɔ:l	Herbst
bonnet **hood**	'bɒnɪt hʊd	Motorhaube
boot **trunk**	bu:t trʌŋk	Kofferraum
caravan **trailer**	'kærəvæn 'treɪlə	Wohnanhänger
chairman **President**	'tʃeəmən 'prezɪdənt	Vorsitzender
pharmacy **drugstore**	'fɑ:məsɪ 'drʌgstɔ:	Apotheke
crisps **chips**	krɪsps tʃɪps	Kartoffelchips
closet	'klɒzɪt	Schrank
curtain **drape**	'kɜ:tən dreɪp	Vorhang
dustbin **garbage can** **trash can**	'dʌstbɪn 'gɑ:bɪdʒ kæn 'træʃ kæn	Abfalleimer
full stop **period**	fʊl stɒp 'pɪərɪəd	Punkt
handbag **purse**	'hændbæg pɜ:s	Handtasche
lift **elevator**	lɪft 'elɪveɪtə	Aufzug, Lift
motorway **freeway**	'məʊtəweɪ 'fri:weɪ	Autobahn
parcel **package**	'pɑ:sl 'pækɪdʒ	Päckchen
pavement **sidewalk**	'peɪvmənt 'saɪdwɔ:k	Bürgersteig

petrol	ˈpetrəl	Benzin
gas	gæs	
tube	tju:b	U-Bahn
subway	ˈsʌbweɪ	
do the dishes	du: ðə ˈdɪʃɪz	abwaschen
Halloween	hæləʊˈi:n	(Abend vor Allerheiligen)
in costume	ɪn ˈkɒstju:m	verkleidet
treat	tri:t	spendieren
shell out	ʃel‿aʊt	etwa: „heraus mit dem Geld"
wrap	ræp	einwickeln
U.N.I.C.E.F.	ˈju:nɪsef	UNICEF
fund	fʌnd	Fond
dress up	dres‿ˈʌp	verkleiden
Roman	ˈrəʊmən	Römer
honour (v)	ˈɒnə	ehren
goddess	ˈgɒdɪs	Göttin
feast	fi:st	Fest
in honour of	ɪn‿ˈɒnər‿əv	zu Ehren von
Christian	ˈkrɪstjən	Christ
saint	seɪnt	Heiliger
nowadays	ˈnaʊədeɪz	heutzutage
witch	wɪtʃ	Hexe
broomstick	ˈbru:mstɪk	Besenstiel
clean out	kli:n‿ˈaʊt	aushöhlen
pumpkin	ˈpʌmpkɪn	Kürbis

Project 5 – Starters

violence	ˈvaɪələns	Gewalt
aggressiveness	əˈgresɪvnɪs	Aggressivität, Angriffslust
crowd	kraʊd	Menge
fault	fɔ:lt	Fehler
reborn	ˈri:bɔ:n	wiedergeboren
leopard	ˈlepəd	Leopard
several	ˈsevrəl	einige
multiple choice	ˈmʌltɪpl ˈtʃɔɪs	Mehrfachauswahl
analyse	ˈænəlaɪz	untersuchen
hell's angel	helz‿ˈeɪndʒəl	Höllenengel (Wappen einer Rockergruppe)
jail	dʒeɪl	ins Gefängnis bringen
bearded	ˈbɪədɪd	bärtig
guilty	ˈgɪltɪ	schuldig
attempt (v)	əˈtempt	versuchen
murder	ˈmɜ:də	Mord
sentence	ˈsentəns	Urteil
total (v)	ˈtəʊtl	insgesamt ergeben
slap on	slæp‿ˈɒn	hier: „aufbrummen"
trial	ˈtraɪəl	Gerichts-verhandlung
clothe, clad, clad	kləʊð, klæd, klæd	(be)kleiden
thug	θʌg	Rowdy
chapter	ˈtʃæptə	hier: Untergruppe einer Vereinigung
federation	fedəˈreɪʃn	Bund, Vereinigung
gang	gæŋ	Bande
mob	mɒb	Pöbel
attack (v)	əˈtæk	angreifen
shotgun	ˈʃɒtgʌn	Schrotflinte
bar	bɑ:	Stange

survive	səˈvaɪv	überleben
raider	ˈreɪdə	Angreifer
shooting	ˈʃu:tɪŋ	Schießerei
aggressor	əˈgresə	Angreifer
obey	əˈbeɪ	gehorchen

Project 5 – Violence

1.

aggressometer	əgreˈsɒmi:tə	Aggressionsmesser
rank order	ræŋk‿ˈɔ:də	Rangordnung
furious	ˈfjʊerɪəs	wütend
cool	ku:l	kühl, ruhig
irate	aɪˈreɪt	zornig
ill-tempered	ˈɪltempəd	schlecht gelaunt
self-controlled	self kənˈtrəʊld	beherrscht
rock music	rɒk ˈmju:zɪk	Rockmusik
flat (adj)	flæt	platt

2.

robber	ˈrɒbə	Räuber
clerk	klɑ:k	Angestellter

3.

sunset	ˈsʌnset	Sonnenuntergang
search (v)	sɜ:tʃ	durchsuchen
rummage	ˈrʌmɪdʒ	wühlen
strip	strɪp	ausziehen
detainee	di:teɪˈni:	Festgenommener
sigh (v)	saɪ	seufzen
remove	rɪˈmu:v	entfernen
pants	pænts	Unterhosen (brit.)
anger	ˈæŋgə	Ärger
well up	wel‿ˈʌp	hochsteigen
control	kənˈtrəʊl	unter Kontrolle bringen
silence	ˈsaɪləns	Stille, Schweigen
fellow	ˈfeləʊ	hier: Kamerad, Mit-
attention	əˈtenʃn	Aufmerksamkeit
cock (v)	kɒk	(Gewehrhahn) spannen
machine gun	məˈʃi:n gʌn	Maschinengewehr
pride	praɪd	Stolz
injure	ˈɪndʒə	verletzen
undress	ʌnˈdres	(sich) ausziehen
prisoner	ˈprɪznə	Gefangener
physical exercise	fɪzɪkəl‿ˈeksəsaɪz	Leibesübungen
bath	bɑ:θ	Bad
pray	preɪ	beten

4.

justice	ˈdʒʌstɪs	Gerechtigkeit
lawyer	ˈlɔ:jə	Rechtsanwalt
legal aid	ˈli:gl‿eɪd	Rechtshilfe
case	keɪs	Fall
serious	ˈsɪərɪəs	ernst
obligation	ɒblɪˈgeɪʃn	Verpflichtung
your Honour	jɔ:r ˈɒnə	Euer Ehren
motion	ˈməʊʃn	Antrag
offence	əˈfens	Vergehen
theft	θeft	Diebstahl
defence attorney	dɪˈfens əˈtɜ:nɪ	Verteidiger
be aware of	bɪ‿əˈweər‿əv	sich klar sein über

5.

list (v)	lıst	auflisten
program	ˈprəʊgræm	Programm
prime time	praım taım	hier: Hauptsendezeit
network	ˈnetwɜ:k	Sendernetz
criminal drama	ˈkrımınl ˈdræmə	Kriminalfilm
comedy	ˈkɒmıdı	Komödie
musical	ˈmju:zıkəl	Musical, Musik-
action	ˈækʃən	Handlung
puzzle	ˈpʌzl	Puzzle, Geduldsspiel
aggression	əˈgreʃən	Aggression
blood	blʌd	Blut
film	fılm	Film
criminal (n)	ˈkrımınl	Verbrecher
finding	ˈfaındıŋ	Fund, Entdeckung
turn on	tɜ:n‿ɒn	hier: heißmachen, aufputschen
mind (v)	maınd	sich kümmern um
disgusting	dısˈgʌstıŋ	ekelhaft
fascinating	ˈfæsıneıtıŋ	faszinierend, fesselnd

Project 5 – Focus on Germany

exclusive	ıksˈklu:sıv	exklusiv, besonders
individual	ındıˈvıdjʊəl	individuell, Einzel-
traveller	ˈtrævlə	Reisender
appreciate	əˈpri:ʃıeıt	schätzen
comfort	ˈkʌmfət	Komfort
convenience	kənˈvi:njəns	Bequemlichkeit
unique	ju:ˈni:k	einzigartig
enchanting	ınˈtʃɑ:ntıŋ	bezaubernd
enable	ıˈneıbl	ermöglichen
conventional	kənˈvenʃənl	konventionell, üblich
bike (v)	baık	Fahrrad fahren
upper Rhine valley	ˈʌpə‿raın ˈvælı	oberes Rheintal
pace	peıs	Gangart, Tempo
accompany	əˈkʌmpənı	begleiten
plus	plʌs	zusätzlich
airfare	ˈeəˈfeə	Flugpreis
romantic	rəʊˈmæntık	romantisch
stagecoach	ˈsteıdʒkəʊtʃ	Postkutsche
landau	ˈlændɔ:	Landauer (offene Kutsche)
landmark	ˈlændmɑ:k	Sehenswürdigkeit
tram	træm	Straßenbahn
S-train	es treın	S-Bahn
fare	ˈfeə	Fahrpreis
valid	ˈvælıd	gültig
cover	ˈkʌvə	hier: gelten für
fine (n)	faın	Geldstrafe
route	ru:t	Strecke
weekly	ˈwi:klı	wöchentlich
monthly	ˈmʌnθlı	monatlich
system	ˈsıstəm	System

Project 5 – Focus on other countries

note	nəʊt	Anmerkung
southern	ˈsʌðən	südlich, Süd-
surface	ˈsɜ:fıs	Oberfläche
yet	jet	hier: dennoch
rarely	ˈreəlı	selten
social	ˈsəʊʃəl	gesellschaftlich
confine	ˈkɒnfaın	begrenzen
community	kəˈmju:nıtı	Gemeinde
vice versa	vaısı ˈvɜ:sə	umgekehrt
terror	ˈterə	Terror, Schrecken
brief	bri:f	kurz
nobleman	ˈnəʊblmən	Adeliger
Anglo-Irish	ˈæŋgləʊ ˈaırıʃ	Anglo-Ire
rule (n)	ru:l	hier: Herrschaft
rebellion	rıˈbeljən	Aufstand
support (n)	səˈpɔ:t	Unterstützung
fleet	fli:t	Flotte
colonize	ˈkɒlənaız	besiedeln
crusade	kru:ˈseıd	Kreuzzug
supporter	səˈpɔ:tə	Anhänger
veteran	ˈvetərən	ehemaliger Soldat
sympathize	ˈsımpəθaız	sympathisieren
French Revolution	frentʃ revəˈlu:ʃən	Französische Revolution
famine	ˈfæmın	Hungersnot
starvation	stɑ:ˈveıʃən	Hungertod
rising	ˈraızıŋ	Erhebung
seat	si:t	Sitz
parliament	ˈpɑ:ləmənt	Parlament
peaceful	ˈpi:sfʊl	friedlich
Nobel Peace Prize	ˈnəʊbəl pi:s praız	Friedensnobelpreis
Orange	ˈɒrındʒ	hier: „Oranier“
ghetto	ˈgetəʊ	Ghetto
arrest (v)	əˈrest	festnehmen
civilian	sıˈvıljən	Zivilist
I.R.A.	ˈaı ˈɑ:r ˈeı	IRA, Irish-Republikanische Armee
cease fire	si:s ˈfaıə	Waffenstillstand
afterwards	ˈɑ:ftəwədz	später
sum up	sʌm‿ʌp	zusammenfassen

Project 5 – Language study package

severe	sıˈvıə	heftig
beating	ˈbi:tıŋ	Schläge, Prügel
mood	mu:d	Stimmung
motorcyclist	ˈməʊtəsaıklıst	Motorradfahrer
oppose	əˈpəʊz	sich entgegenstellen
quarrelsome	ˈkwɒrəlsəm	streitsüchtig
reckless	ˈreklıs	rücksichtslos
consequence	ˈkɒnsıkwəns	Folge
drunk	drʌŋk	betrunken
dash	dæʃ	stürmen, jagen
smooth	smu:ð	sanft, weich
skin	skın	Haut
harsh	hɑ:ʃ	rauh, barsch
unpleasant	ʌnˈpleznt	unangenehm
behaviour	bıˈheıvjə	Benehmen, Verhalten
chase	tʃeıs	jagen
thieve	θi:v	stehlen
able	ˈeıbl	fähig
regret	rıˈgret	bedauern
force (n)	fɔ:s	Macht, Kraft
earthquake	ˈɜ:θkweık	Erdbeben
temper	ˈtempə	Temperament
raging	ˈreıdʒıŋ	wütend, heftig

painful	ˈpeɪnfʊl	schmerzhaft
extreme	ɪksˈtri:m	extrem, außerordentlich
awakening	əˈweɪknɪŋ	Erwachen
surprise	səˈpraɪz	Überraschung

Project 6 – Starters

supernatural	su:pəˈnætʃrəl	das Übernatürliche
middle ages	mɪdl‿ˈeɪdʒɪz	Mittelalter

Project 6 – The supernatural

1.

check	tʃek	überprüfen
fighter plane	ˈfaɪtəpleɪn	Kampfflugzeug
investigate	ɪnˈvestɪgeɪt	untersuchen, erkunden
disappear	dɪsəˈpɪə	verschwinden
U.F.O. (unidentified flying object)	ˈju: fəʊ ʌnaɪˈdentɪfaɪd ˈflaɪɪŋ ˈɒbdʒɪkt	UFO (unidentifiziertes Flugobjekt)
glow	gləʊ	glühen
bright	braɪt	strahlend, hell
balloon	bəˈlu:n	Ballon
atmosphere	ˈætməsfɪə	Atmosphäre
play tricks	pleɪ trɪks	einen Streich spielen
moonlight	ˈmu:nlaɪt	Mondlicht
summary	ˈsʌmərɪ	Zusammenfassung
grid	grɪd	Gitter, Netz
shape	ʃeɪp	Form

2.

farewell	ˈfeəˈwel	Abschied
sleepy	ˈsli:pɪ	schläfrig
doze off	dəʊz‿ˈɒf	eindösen
pat	pæt	Klaps, Klopfen
gentleman	ˈdʒentlmən	Herr
transmitter	trænzˈmɪtə	Sender
on the air	ɒn‿ðɪ‿eə	„auf Sendung"
man (v)	mæn	bemannen
fanatic	fəˈnætɪk	begeisterter Anhänger
radioscope	reɪdɪəʊˈskəʊp	Radiosender
goodlooking	ˈgʊdˈlʊkɪŋ	gutaussehend
accent	ˈæksənt	Akzent
claim (v)	kleɪm	behaupten
actual	ˈæktʃʊəl	tatsächlich
outer	ˈaʊtə	äußere, äußeres
laser beam	ˈleɪzə bi:m	Laserstrahl
herd	hɜ:d	Herde
hide, hid, hidden	haɪd, hɪd, ˈhɪdn	verstecken
headlight	ˈhedlaɪt	Licht, Scheinwerfer
burst, burst, burst	bɜ:st, bɜ:st, bɜ:st	zerbersten
beam	bi:m	Strahl
hum	hʌm	summen
assistant	əˈsɪstənt	Assistent
retell, retold, retold	ri:ˈtel, ri:ˈtəʊld, ri:ˈtəʊld	nacherzählen, wiedergeben
silvery	ˈsɪlvərɪ	silbrig
wave	weɪv	winken
ladder	ˈlædə	Leiter
smile (n)	smaɪl	lächeln
electronics	ɪlekˈtrɒnɪks	Elektronik
receiver	rɪˈsi:və	Empfänger
earphone	ˈɪəfəʊn	Kopfhörer
communication	kəmju:nɪˈkeɪʃən	Verbindung, Verständigung
cry (v)	kraɪ	schreien
code	kəʊd	Code
guest	gest	Gast
pond	pɒnd	Teich
appear	əˈpɪə	erscheinen
descend	dɪˈsend	heruntersteigen
touch (v)	tʌtʃ	berühren
sink, sank, sunk	sɪŋk, sæŋk, sʌŋk	sinken
gobble up	ˈgɒbl‿ʌp	verschlingen
find	faɪnd	Fund
secret	ˈsi:krɪt	geheim

3.

horoscope	ˈhɒrəskəʊp	Horoskop
amulet	ˈæmjʊlɪt	Amulett
wonder	ˈwʌndə	Wunder
talisman	ˈtælɪzmən	Talisman, Glücksbringer
angel	ˈeɪndʒəl	Engel
demon	ˈdi:mən	Dämon
mind reading	ˈmaɪnd ˈri:dɪŋ	Gedankenlesen
evil eye	i:vl‿ˈaɪ	böser Blick
telepathy	tɪˈlepəθɪ	Telepathie
prediction	prɪˈdɪkʃn	Vorhersage
base on	beɪs‿ɒn	sich gründen auf
midnight	ˈmɪdnaɪt	Mitternacht
power	ˈpaʊə	Kraft
bad luck	bæd lʌk	Pech
creature	ˈkri:tʃə	Wesen
quack doctor	kwæk ˈdɒktə	Quacksalber
lay	leɪ	legen
cure (v)	ˈkjʊə	heilen
devil	ˈdevl	Teufel
hell	hel	Hölle

4.

bible	ˈbaɪbl	Bibel
ark	ɑ:k	Arche
unto (= to)	ˈʌntʊ	zu
thee (= you)	ði:	dich, dir
thou (= you)	ðaʊ	du
shalt (= shall)	ʃælt	soll(st)
flood	flʌd	Flut, Überschwemmung
orchestra	ˈɔ:kɪstrə	Orchester
fear	ˈfɪə	Furcht
craziness	ˈkreɪzɪnɪs	Verrücktheit
publicity	pʌbˈlɪsətɪ	Reklame
survival	səˈvaɪvəl	Überleben
instinct	ˈɪnstɪŋkt	Instinkt, Trieb
show off	ʃəʊ‿ɒf	„angeben"
attract	əˈtrækt	anziehen
unhappiness	ʌnˈhæpɪnɪs	Unglück(seligkeit)
creativity	krɪeɪˈtɪvɪtɪ	Kreativität, schöpferisches Talent
spiritual (n)	ˈspɪrɪtjʊəl	geistliches Lied
Lord	lɔ:d	Herr
drop (v)	drɒp	tropfen

'cause (= because)	kɒz (bɪ'kɒz)	weil
moan	məʊn	stöhnen
row (v)	rəʊ	rudern
rescue	'reskju:	retten
on board	ɒn 'bɔ:d	an Bord
Gospel	'gɒspl	Evangelium
at hand	ət 'hænd	ganz nahe
rumble	'rʌmbl	rumpeln
aboard	ə'bɔ:d	an Bord
singer	'sɪŋə	Sänger
Russian	'rʌʃən	Russe, russisch
expedition	ekspɪ'dɪʃn	Expedition
set out	set‿aʊt	sich aufmachen

5.

rectory	'rektərɪ	Pfarrhaus
haunt	hɔ:nt	spuken
monastery	'mɒnəstərɪ	Kloster
monk	mʌŋk	Mönch
fall in love	fɔ:l‿ɪn lʌv	sich verlieben
nun	nʌn	Nonne
nearby	'nɪəbaɪ	nahelegen
nunnery	'nʌnərɪ	Nonnenkloster
escape	ɪ'skeɪp	entkommen
coach	kəʊtʃ	Kutsche
hang, hanged, hanged	hæŋ, hæŋd, hæŋd	hängen
wall up	wɔ:l‿ʌp	einmauern
sad	sæd	traurig
phantom	'fæntəm	Geist
race (v)	reɪs	rasen
kidnap	'kɪdnæp	entführen
owner	'əʊnə	Besitzer
reverend	'revərənd	Geistlicher
vicar	'vɪkə	Vikar
gloomy	'glu:mɪ	düster
frequent	'fri:kwənt	häufig
brick up	brɪk‿ʌp	zumauern
occasion	ə'keɪʒn	Gelegenheit
glide	glaɪd	gleiten
figure (n)	'fɪgə	Figur, Gestalt
passage	'pæsɪdʒ	Gang
haunting	'hɔ:ntɪŋ	Spuk
church warden	'tʃɜ:tʃ 'wɔ:dn	Küster
robe	rəʊb	Gewand
shy (v)	ʃaɪ	scheuen
snort	snɔ:t	schnauben
lane	leɪn	Weg
disappear into thin air	dɪsə'pɪər‿ɪntu θɪn eə	sich in Luft auflösen
occupant	'ɒkjʊpənt	Bewohner
old-fashioned	əʊld'fæʃnd	altmodisch
box seat	bɒks si:t	Kutschbock
veterinary	'vetərɪnərɪ	Tierarzt
realize	'rɪəlaɪz	erkennen
puddle	'pʌdl	Pfütze
stroll	strəʊl	spazierengehen
researcher	rɪ'sɜ:tʃə	Forscher

6.

fable	'feɪbl	Fabel
Christ	kraɪst	Christus
frog	frɒg	Frosch
cure (n)	'kjʊə	Kur
do away	du:‿ə'weɪ	abschaffen, beseitigen
disease	dɪ'zi:z	Krankheit
promise	'prɒmɪs	versprechen
heal	hi:l	heilen
lame	leɪm	lahm
moral	'mɒrəl	Moral
be about to	bi: ə'baʊt tu	vorhaben, im Begriff sein (etwas zu tun)
invite	ɪn'vaɪt	einladen
banquet	'bæŋkwɪt	Festmahl
crush	krʌʃ	zerquetschen, zerdrücken
double (v)	'dʌbl	verdoppeln
kick	kɪk	treten
smash	smæʃ	zertrümmern, zerstampfen
helpless	'helplɪs	hilflos
discord	'dɪskɔ:d	Zwietracht, Uneinigkeit
swell up	swel‿ʌp	anschwellen
wasp	wɒsp	Wespe
snake	sneɪk	Schlange
sting, stung, stung	stɪŋ, stʌŋ, stʌŋ	stechen
cost	kɒst	Kosten
contents	'kɒntents	Inhalt
nevertheless	nevəðə'les	dennoch
meaningful	'mi:nɪŋfʊl	bedeutungsvoll
by heart	baɪ hɑ:t	auswendig

Project 6 – Focus on Germany

contact (v)	kən'tækt	in Verbindung treten
waiting list	'weɪtɪŋ lɪst	Warteliste
Red Cross	red krɒs	Rotes Kreuz
demand	dɪ'mɑ:nd	verlangen
take turns	teɪk tɜ:nz	sich abwechseln
indicate	'ɪndɪkeɪt	anzeigen
expense	ɪk'spens	Kosten

Project 6 – Focus on other countries

precede	prɪ'si:d	vorhergehen
caste	keɪst	Kaste
aspect	'æspekt	Gesichtspunkt
trader	'treɪdə	Händler
merchant	'mɜ:tʃənt	Kaufmann
skilled	skɪld	ausgebildet
Pariah	'pærɪə	Paria
so-called	'səʊ kɔ:ld	sogenannt
untouchable	ʌn'tʌtʃəbl	unberührbar
break down	breɪk daʊn	hier: niederreißen
barrier	'bærɪə	Barriere, Schranke
abolish	ə'bɒlɪʃ	abschaffen
despite	dɪs'paɪt	trotz
developing country	dɪ'veləpɪŋ 'kʌntrɪ	Entwicklungsland
plant	plɑ:nt	Fabrik
founder	'faʊndə	Gründer
admire	əd'maɪə	bewundern
institution	ɪnstɪ'tju:ʃən	Einrichtung
fair play	'feə 'pleɪ	Fairneß, Anständigkeit

Project 7 – Starters

absolute	'æbsəlu:t	unbedingt
warmth	wɔ:mθ	Wärme
arrange	ə'reɪndʒ	anordnen
physical	'fɪzɪkl	körperlich
soul	səʊl	Seele
precaution	prɪ'kɔ:ʃn	Vorsichts-maßnahme
provide	prə'vaɪd	bereitstellen
thunderstorm	'θʌndəstɔ:m	Gewitter
shed	ʃed	Schuppen
fence	fens	Zaun
pylon	'paɪlən	Hochspannungs-mast
isolated	aɪsə'leɪtɪd	alleinstehend, isoliert
seek, sought, sought	si:k, sɔ:t, sɔ:t	suchen
hollow (n)	'hɒləʊ	Senke
ground	graʊnd	Boden
overhanging	'əʊvəhæŋɪŋ	überhängend
cliff	klɪf	Klippe
touch (v)	tʌtʃ	berühren

Project 7 – Survival

1.

slum	slʌm	Elendsviertel
coin	kɔɪn	Münze
plantation	plæn'teɪʃn	Plantage
temperate	'tempərət	gemäßigt
tropic	'trɒpɪk	tropisch
characteristic (n)	kærɪktə'rɪstɪk	Merkmal
savannah	sə'vænə	Savanne
humid	'hju:mɪd	feucht
tropical	'trɒpɪkl	tropisch
pine	paɪn	Fichte
snow	snəʊ	Schnee
livestock	'laɪvstɒk	Viehbestand
deciduous	dɪ'sɪdjʊəs	Laub-
steppe	step	Steppe
tundra	'tʌndrə	Tundra
permanent	'pɜ:mənənt	dauernd
frost	frɒst	Frost

2.

doorway	'dɔ:weɪ	Türöffnung
childbirth	'tʃaɪldbɜ:θ	Entbindung
meanwhile	'mi:nwaɪl	inzwischen
CCF	'si:'si: 'ef	Abkürzung für Christian Children's Fund
sponsor (n, v)	'spɒnsə	Förderer, Pate, fördern
opportunity	ɒpə'tju:nɪtɪ	Möglichkeit
priceless	'praɪslɪs	unbezahlbar
intimate	'ɪntɪmɪt	eng, innig
blessing	'blesɪŋ	Segnung
youngster	'jʌŋstə	junger Mensch
urgent	'ɜ:dʒənt	dringend
select	sɪ'lekt	auswählen

3.

blow, blew blown	bləʊ, blu:, bləʊn	blasen
railway	'reɪlweɪ	Eisenbahn
bench	bentʃ	Bank
fitful	'fɪtfʊl	unruhig
sleep (n)	sli:p	Schlaf
interrupt	ɪntə'rʌpt	unterbrechen
hostel	'hɒstl	Herberge
sleep rough	sli:p rʌf	im Freien schlafen
lodgings	'lɒdʒɪŋz	Privatquartier
tumor	tju:mə	Tumor, Geschwulst
brain	breɪn	Gehirn
cell	sel	Zelle
married	'mærɪd	verheiratet
stick (v)	stɪk	aushalten
tolerate	'tɒləreɪt	ertragen
lampshade	'læmpʃeɪd	Lampenschirm
a couple of	ə‿'kʌpl‿əv	ein paar
be not supposed to	bɪ nɒt sə'pəʊzd tə	nicht dürfen, sollen
allow	ə'laʊ	erlauben
lodger	'lɒdʒə	zahlender Gast, Untermieter
chuck out	tʃʌk‿aʊt	hinauswerfen

4.

Jewish	'dʒu:ɪʃ	jüdisch
missus (= Missis)	'mɪsɪz	Frau
encourage	ɪn'kʌrɪdʒ	ermutigen
transport	'trænspɔ:t	befördern
brave	breɪv	tapfer
Moor	'mʊə	Mohr

5.

statistic	stə'tɪstɪk	Statistik
technology	tek'nɒlədʒɪ	Technologie
advance	əd'vɑ:ns	Fortschritt
decade	'dekeɪd	Jahrzehnt
soil	sɔɪl	(Erd)boden
liquid	'lɪkwɪd	flüssig
farm (v)	fɑ:m	bebauen
beneath	bɪ'ni:θ	unter
Ministry of Agriculture and Fisheries	'mɪnɪstrɪ‿əv ægrɪ'kʌltʃər‿ənd 'fɪʃərɪz	Ministerium für Landwirtschaft und Fischereiwesen
hectare	'hektɑ:	Hektar
available	ə'veɪləbl	verfügbar
develop	dɪ'veləp	entwickeln

6.

optimistic	ɒptɪ'mɪstɪk	optimistisch
pessimistic	pesɪ'mɪstɪk	pessimistisch
relaxation	ri:læk'seɪʃn	Entspannung
volcano	vɒl'keɪnəʊ	Vulkan
classify	'klæsɪfaɪ	einstufen
likely	'laɪklɪ	wahrscheinlich
optimist	'ɒptɪmɪst	Optimist
pessimist	'pesɪmɪst	Pessimist

Project 7 – Focus on Germany

novel	'nɒvəl	Roman
witty	'wɪtɪ	geistvoll
capital letter	'kæpɪtl 'letə	Großbuchstabe
confuse	kən'fju:z	verwirren
translate	træns'leɪt	übersetzen
length	leŋθ	Länge

perspective	pə'spektɪv	Perspektive
alphabetical	ælfə'betɪkl	alphabetisch
procession	prə'seʃn	Prozession
majestical	mə'dʒestɪkl	majestätisch
valuable	'væljʊəbl	wertvoll
tramp	træmp	Tramp, Landstreicher

Project 7 – Focus on other countries

totem-pole	'təʊtəm pəʊl	Totenpfahl
canoeing	kə'nu:ɪŋ	Kanufahren
elk	elk	Elch
uninhabited	'ʌnɪn'hæbɪtɪd	unbewohnt
immigration	ɪmɪ'greɪʃən	Einwanderung
proclaim	prə'kleɪm	verkünden
regulate	'regjʊleɪt	regeln
for good	fə gʊd	für immer
temporary	'tempərərɪ	zeitweise
worker	'wɜ:kə	Arbeiter
immigrate	'ɪmɪgreɪt	einwandern
relative	'relətɪv	Verwandter
sponsor (v)	'spɒnsə	bürgen
refugee	'refjʊdʒi:	Flüchtling
asylant	ə'saɪlənt	Asylsuchender
qualify	'kwɒlɪfaɪ	Eignung nachweisen
citizenship	'sɪtɪznʃɪp	Staatsangehörigkeit
regular	'regjʊlə	normal, vorschriftsmäßig
applicant	'æplɪkənt	Antragsteller
knowledge	'nɒlɪdʒ	Kenntnisse, Wissen
right	raɪt	Recht
responsibility	rɪspɒnsə'bɪlɪtɪ	Verantwortlichkeit
apply for	ə'plaɪ fɔ:	beantragen
hearing	'hɪərɪŋ	Anhörung, Vernehmung
attend	ə'tend	teilnehmen, beiwohnen
oath	əʊθ	Eid

Contents

Project seven: Survival

Quellenverzeichnis

S. 32: Aus Dictionary of Word and Phrase Origins von William and Mary Morris, Harper & Row, New York 1962

S. 44: „Wo nur die Macht zählt" aus Die Welt, 7. Oktober 1980

S. 45: "William Spotted Horse" von J. Schütt, Aurich

S. 54 f.: "What happened at Wounded Knee?" aus The New York Times, December 30, 1890 bzw. February 12, 1891

S. 68: "The boy who invented the Bubble Gun" von Paul Gallico aus dem gleichnamigen Buch, Dell Publishing Co. New York

S. 74: "The Marine Chronometer" aus Edward de Bono, Eureka, 1974, London (Bearbeitung)

8. 87: "Crazy Hell's Angel is jailed 15 Years" aus The Sun, March 28, 1980

S. 96: "Wunder Adventures in Germany" von Deutsche Zentrale für Touismus EV., New York

S. 112 ff.: "Borley Rectory" aus P. Underwood, Hauntings, London (Bearbeitet)

S. 126: "Hunger is all she has ever known" mit freundlicher Genehmigung des Christian Children's Funds, Richmond, Va.

S. 127: "Nowhere to call home" von Sandra Grant in The Sunday Telegraph, quoted from Alan Duff: That's Life, Cambridge University Press 1979

S. 128: "The green Years" von Peter Abrahams aus Modern African Prose

S. 132: "The awful German language" adapted from Mark Twain "A Tramp Abroad"

Bildnachweis

Bavaria/Ric – S. 117 (1)
Bavaria/Schmied – S. 133 (1, 2)
dpa – S. 98, 115
Levi Strauss & Co., San Francisco – S. 32, 33
National Museum, Grenwich – S. 73
Okapia – S. 133 (3, 4)
Deutsche Zentrale für Tourismus E.V. – S. 96
Piepho Archiv – S. 105
United States Information Service – S. 42, 46/47
V-Dia, Heidelberg – S. 58
Zefa – S. 35 (1, 2, 3, 4), 103, 126
V-Dia, Heidelberg – S. 59 (1, 2, 3)
Aus e. o. plauen: Vater und Sohn, Bd. 2, Otto Maier Verlag, Ravensburg – S. 89
Aus J. Payne: All in the mind, Oxford University Press – S. 109
Aus Focus on Facts – The Psychic World, Allen & Co, London – S. 112
Aus Ure Smith: This is Australia – S. 59 (1)
Aus R. B. Hassrick: The American West – S. 43

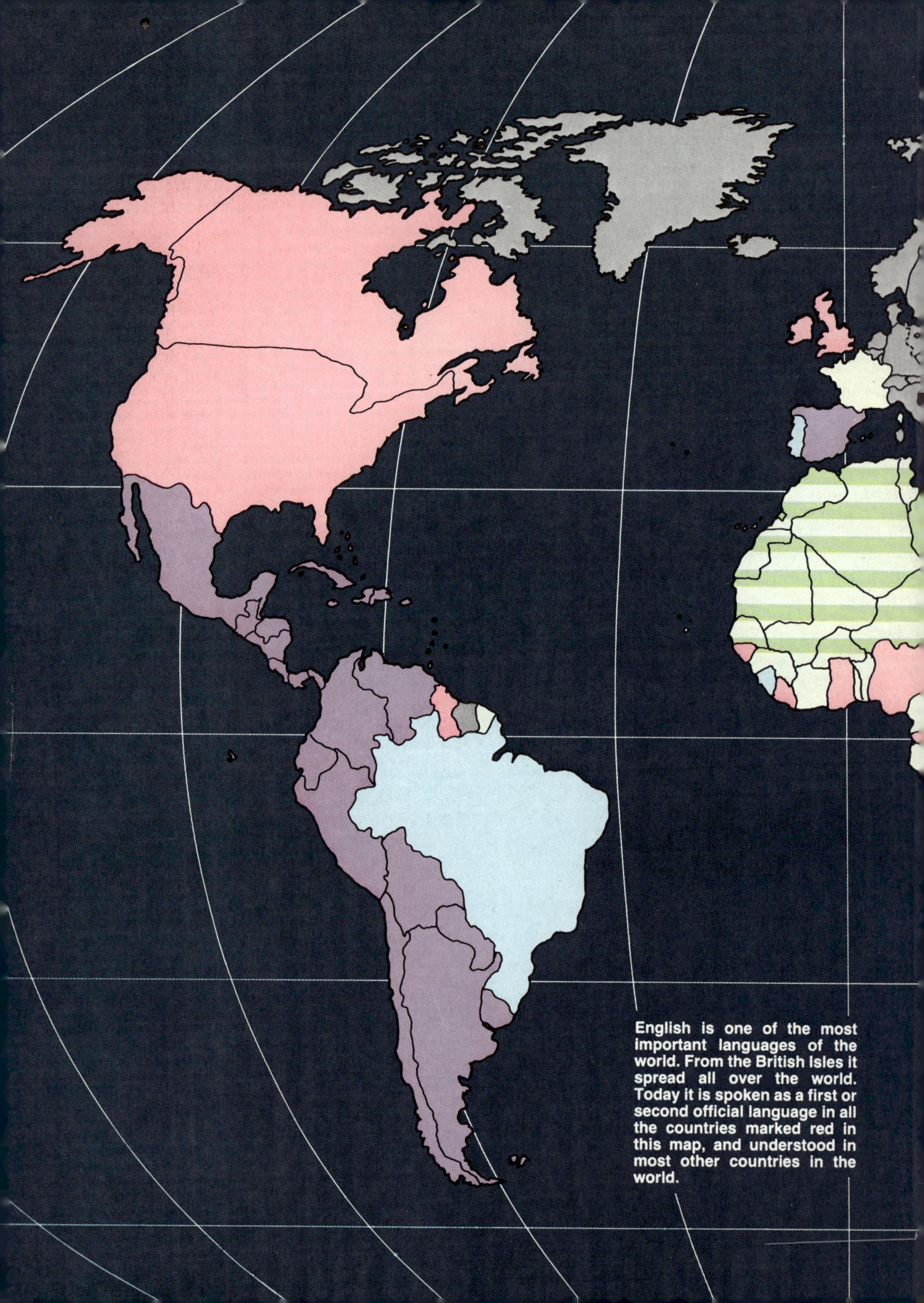

English is one of the most important languages of the world. From the British Isles it spread all over the world. Today it is spoken as a first or second official language in all the countries marked red in this map, and understood in most other countries in the world.